BLOODY BRITISH HISTORY

# SHREWSBURY

## DOROTHY NICOLLE

The History Press

Unless otherwise credited, all pictures are from either the author's or the publisher's collection.

First published in 2013

The History Press
The Mill, Brimscombe Port
Stroud, Gloucestershire, GL5 2QG
www.thehistorypress.co.uk

British Library Cataloguing in Publication Data.
A catalogue record for this book is available from the British Library.

ISBN 978 0 7524 8270 5

Typesetting and origination by The History Press
Printed in Great Britain

# CONTENTS

# THE ROMANS ARRIVE IN SHROPSHIRE

SOON AFTER THEIR invasion, the Roman army reached Shropshire – not that it was called Shropshire in those days. This was then the territory of a tribe called the Cornovii. Those Celtic tribes were a warlike lot, always fighting, rustling each other's cattle, stealing each other's women – and goodness knows what else. In all probability when the Romans invaded Britannia and landed in the south-east of the country in AD 43, the tribe of the Cornovii would have taken little notice – at first.

Having established a foothold, however, the Romans began to take control, steadily working their way north and west, subduing individual tribes as they went. But not everyone was prepared to submit. One such Celt was a man who has come to be known to history as Caratacus (although in the Celtic language of the day his name was probably something akin to 'Caradoc'). His father surrendered to the Romans but there was no way that Caratacus was going to follow suit. Instead, he carried out a guerilla-style fight for freedom; but against such a mighty war machine his forces had little hope of success, and he was instead pushed ever westwards.

Eventually the Romans managed to force Caratacus to meet them in a full-scale battle somewhere in the region that we now know as Shropshire and, sure enough, Caratacus was defeated. But in the mayhem that followed the defeat Caratacus managed to escape and fled to the North, where he took refuge with another Celtic tribe, the Brigantes.

The Roman army worked its inevitable way north and finally forced the Brigantes, too, to surrender. As part of the peace treaty the Brigantes were forced to hand Caratacus over to the Romans and he was then taken to Rome, where he was paraded, in irons, through the streets of that city. And that should have been the end of him.

But it wasn't.

Instead, Caratacus so impressed the Romans with the dignity and courage with which he put up with every trial they could throw at him that, in the end, they decided to spare him. Obviously he could never be allowed to return to Britannia, where we would have been a focus for any possible future rebellion,

## LARGER EVEN THAN YORK

The Roman town of Viroconium (or Wroxeter, as it is now known) that preceded Shrewsbury was the fourth largest town in all of Roman Britain, larger even than Chester, just up the road, York or Lincoln.

In case you are wondering what the first three were – they were London, Cirencester and St Albans.

*The ruins of Wroxeter, sketched in around the 1900s.*

so, instead, he was allowed to live in relative comfort in what today we would describe as a form of 'house-arrest' until he eventually died a natural death.

The important thing about Caratacus is that he is our first truly documented British hero. And where did that battle take place? We just don't know. Was it at the hill-fort that bears his name, Caer Caradoc, near Church Stretton? Or was it, as archaeologists now tend to think, on the hill-fort at Llanymynech?

# THE RESCUE OF ST ALKMUND'S BONES

**O**NE OF THE earliest churches founded in Shrewsbury was dedicated to a Northumbrian saint, St Alkmund, who quite possibly never had anything to do with the town. Well – not when he was alive, at least.

St Alkmund was probably born in around the 770s. He was the son of King Alcred of Northumbria and was well known for his charitable acts towards the poor and orphaned. His father and elder brother were murdered and so Alkmund fled to Scotland – where agents of Eardwulf (who had usurped the throne) found and murdered him, too, probably in around AD 800 (some reports say 819).

One hundred or so years later, the people of England suffered from a constant fear of attack from Viking raiders. With their low-draught boats the Vikings could venture far inland, using the rivers, so that it was not just the coastal areas that were at risk. Indeed, they once wintered as far upstream as present-day Bridgnorth, and from landing sites like that it was no hardship for them to steal a few horses and go marauding even further inland.

## HOW DO YOU PRONOUNCE SHREWSBURY?

Do you say 'Shrowesbury' or do you say 'Shrewsbury'? Which is right? To tell the truth, it is difficult to say. Over the years there have been numerous variations in the way the name of the town is spelt in documents and, presumably, the clerks writing it down were attempting to write phonetically whatever it is they heard. We've had Scrobbesbyrig and Schrossysbury, Shrovesbury and Shrowesbury – to mention just a few.

Local tradition has it that the earlier pronunciation was closer to 'Shrow' than to 'Shrew'. Notice how all the above versions have an 'o' in them. Then, so the story goes, at some time someone made a spelling mistake and missed out that 'o' and so, from that day to this, people have argued about how to say the word.

Mind you, things are only going to get worse. These days many local people say neither Shrow nor Shrew but say Shoesbury instead...

# A PRECARIOUS SEAT FOR THE DEVIL

The steeple of St Alkmund's church is said, by the people of Shrewsbury, to be used by the Devil as a lookout point. Sitting up there he has an excellent view of the countryside around and, particularly, of the Stiperstone Hills to the south. It is also said that all the ghosts of Shropshire meet once a year, on the longest night of the year, and the Devil chairs this meeting sitting in one of the rock formations on the Stiperstones known as The Devil's Chair.

It would appear that the Devil is very possessive about that chair and, when he sits on St Alkmund's spire, should he see someone sitting in it, he promptly sends a thunder and lightning storm to frighten such upstarts away.

I'm always curious as to where such strange stories come from, and there seems to be a clear origin for this story. Apparently, in the 1550s there was a severe storm over the town during which lightning struck St Alkmund's. The following day the townspeople went to inspect any possible damage and discovered that the strike had hit a bell within the church tower, causing what looked very much like a claw mark down the side of the bell. Was this caused by the Devil's talon?

*St Alkmund's church and spire today.*

The burgh town of Scrobbesbyrig, however, was deemed to be relatively safe when the Vikings, pictured above, were attacking lands further to the east, along valleys such as that of the River Trent. And so it's quite possible that the bones of a saint such as St Alkmund, who had been buried in Derbyshire, could have been brought here for safety. The problem is that we just don't know for certain, though this does seem to be the most likely explanation of why a church here should be dedicated to him.

The establishment of burgh towns such as Scrobbesbyrig had been an innovation of King Alfred. Waging constant war against the Vikings, Alfred soon realised that they were seeking easily portable plunder. If people could take refuge in strongly fortified towns, the Vikings might lay waste to stretches of the countryside around but find little to satisfy them in terms of portable wealth and would therefore, it was hoped, leave all the sooner to seek out easier pickings elsewhere. The strategy was relatively successful and Alfred established many burgh towns all through his territory of Wessex.

Subsequently, after King Alfred married off his daughter, Ethelflaeda, to King Leofric, who ruled the realm of Mercia, Alfred's strategy was followed throughout Mercia too. Indeed, when Leofric died, Ethelflaeda ruled in her own name and continued this policy. Ethelflaeda founded a number of castles – Warwick, Stafford, Hereford and Runcorn amongst them. It has been suggested that she also founded the first castle in Scrobbesbyrig but, unfortunately, there would appear to be no evidence, either on the ground or in documentary sources, to prove this.

# WILD EADRIC ATTACKS SHREWSBURY

**MUCH OF WHAT** we know of this period in Shrewsbury's history comes to us from a historian with the wonderful name of Ordericus Vitalis. He was born in 1075 just a couple of miles from Shrewsbury in the village of Atcham, his father (a French priest) having come to Shropshire in the retinue of Roger de Montgomery.

At the age of five, Ordericus (or Orderic) began his education with an English priest named Siward. The boy must have shown some promise because, aged eleven, he was then sent to Normandy, where he entered the monastery of St Evroul-en-Ouche. It is said that his father paid the enormous sum of thirty marks in order to get the boy admitted. From then on Ordericus was linked to the French monastery, although he is known to have travelled occasionally – and even returned to England at least once. Though he spent most of his life in France and had a French father, he seems always to have considered himself first and foremost to be an Englishman. Unable to speak the French language when he first arrived

in Normandy, he describes, in one of his works, how he felt like a stranger in France – he was obviously very homesick for England and never lost his attachment to the country of his birth.

Today, Ordericus Vitalis is best known for his *Historia Ecclesiastica*, a history that, in a number of volumes, describes, amongst other things, the Norman conquests of both England and southern Italy. He has been described in recent years as 'an honest and trustworthy guide to the history of his times'.

Ordericus certainly had a lot to record in this era, including the Norman Conquest in 1066 – and the many revolts that followed it. Many English lords led a resistance against the Norman invaders. The best known of these eleventh-century resistance fighters is Hereward the Wake, who fought from his stronghold in the Isle of Ely. There were many others ranging as far afield as Yorkshire to the West Country but, sadly, they seem never to have found a single leader who could pull them all together to make their resistance effective. Wild Eadric was one such Saxon warlord. He is known to have owned at least six manors in Shropshire and one in Herefordshire at the time of the Norman invasion. Amazingly, he was allowed to retain his lands after the Conquest, so we can only assume that he was not present at the Battle of Hastings – indeed, Vitalis tells us that he submitted to King William at, or soon after, the new King's coronation.

Any good feeling was not to last. No sooner had he gained control of England than William started to hand out parcels of land to his Norman mercenaries. Amongst such Normans was Roger de Montgomery, who was given control over what is today much of Shropshire, Herefordshire and Montgomeryshire. Roger then, in turn, handed out smaller sections of his new territories to his own supporters, and it was not long before these men started to encroach on those few Saxon lords, such as Eadric, who still had their own lands. It was inevitable that trouble would ensue.

As early as 1067, after raids on his lands by Norman neighbours, an exasperated Eadric allied himself to two Welsh Princes and rebelled, attacking Hereford and then retreating into the safety of the Welsh hills. It was probably around this time that he was given the nickname of *Silvaticus* or wild. Today we would understand this to mean that he had a wild personality; it is much more likely, though, that it means that he lived wild, as a rebel, hiding in the forests and hills, an outlaw constantly attacking and plundering the newly-arrived Normans.

The attacks continued and, in 1069, Eadric took advantage of the fact that William was otherwise engaged fighting in northern England, and attacked Shrewsbury.

William, having laid waste to much of Yorkshire, then moved south-west to deal with this new problem. A combined English-Welsh force was defeated by William at Stafford but Wild Eadric himself escaped, once again, into the hills.

History does not tell us what then happened. All we know for certain is that Eadric somehow fell into Norman hands, and that he seems to have come to some arrangement with William I: in 1072, he even accompanied William on campaign in Scotland. But this alliance was not to last: in 1075, he is thought to have been involved in yet another rebellion and may then have lost the last of his lands.

## THE GHOST OF WILD EADRIC

Inevitably a number of legends have arisen associated with Wild Eadric. History does not tell us where or when he died, but tradition in Shropshire has it that he lies buried somewhere in the lead mines of the Stiperstones Hills – and that his ghost roams the hills to this day. Whenever he appears, riding his warhorse, it is said to be a warning that the country will soon be at war. He is said to have been seen in the months before the Crimean War broke out, and before both the First and Second World Wars. He is also said to have been seen before the Falklands War, but I have heard no mention of him appearing before either of the recent Gulf Wars.

Incidentally, if, when you are walking in the hills, you should happen to see Wild Eadric, you must count the number

# THE EXPLODING CONQUEROR!

There is a stone-cut sarcophagus beside St Julian's church. No one knows who it is made for, or whether or not it was ever used. Coffins such as this one were a regular feature in medieval times (although, of course, it was only the wealthy who could afford one). There must have been times, however, when wealthy people were caught short – dying before their favoured stonemason could measure them up properly and prepare the coffin to fit. Perhaps the most famous person to suffer such an inconvenience was King William the Conqueror, who died in 1087.

William was fatally injured in a riding accident when overseeing the besieging of the castle at Mantes in France. Over the next few weeks he writhed in agony as various physicians tried to save his life, whilst the monks persuaded him to atone for

*The empty sarcophagus.*

all his sins before he died. The moment he died William was abandoned, enabling the servants to seize what they could – the King's body soon lay almost naked on the floor.

His funeral followed, held in the newly consecrated abbey in Caen. The masons had done their work and set up the coffin in the church; the congregation assembled and, finally, William's body was carried in on a bier and the priests carefully laid him to rest in his newly cut stone box. It was only then that they realised they had a problem: the body was too big to fit the hollowed-out sarcophagus.

Then, in full view of the (not terribly distraught) mourners, one of the priests clambered up on to the stone plinth and proceeded to push down hard on the bloated corpse, doing his best to squash it and squeeze it in. But in so doing he smashed William's ribs so that they punctured his stomach and broke through his flesh. William's body had already started to putrefy. Being suddenly eviscerated in this way caused a noxious pong to rapidly spread through the entire church; it was so ghastly that the entire congregation fled from the building in horror.

*Stiperstones, where Wild Eadric is rumoured to be buried.*

of hunting dogs that run with him – this will tell you just how many years the war will go on for.

As with many other legendary freedom fighters, it is said that Wild Eadric will come back to life once again – in his case, when England has an English King on the throne. Consider this for a moment – those Normans and Plantagenets came from France. Then came the Tudors: they were Welsh, and to a Saxon lord this was probably even worse. The Scottish Stuarts – just as bad as the Welsh to a man like Eadric. The Hanoverians were German. Our present Queen? Well, she is descended from Germans in one line and Scots on the other, probably not good enough for Wild Eadric. The same could be said for Prince Charles. One wonders if Prince William will be considered English enough to suit the Wild Earl?

# SAINT'S BONES BROUGHT TO SHREWSBURY ABBEY

**S**HREWSBURY ABBEY WAS founded by Roger de Montgomery in 1083. Just as many attractions today are dependent on tourists for their income, so, in the past, religious centres were dependent for a large proportion of their incomes on pilgrims. But any religious centre without a saint's shrine had no hope of attracting pilgrims and their associated cash.

As a new foundation, Shrewsbury Abbey had no saintly connections. The monks decided to rectify this omission.

They looked at all the saints within Shropshire, into the borderlands with Wales and deeper into the Principality and came up with a saint who, they thought, would suit them nicely. Dedicated and pure, St Winifred had lived in the mid-seventh century and, even better, the whereabouts of her grave were known. It would thus be possible to collect her bones and bring them to Shrewsbury for presentation to the masses in a magnificent shrine. That would surely attract the pilgrims.

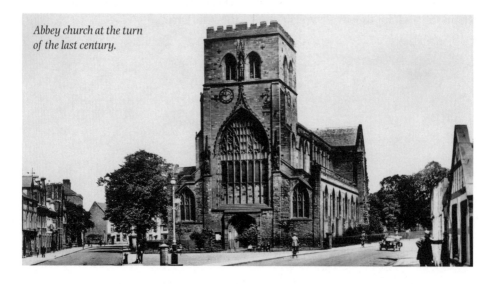

*Abbey church at the turn of the last century.*

Consequently, in 1137, a group of monks from Shrewsbury set off into the wilds of Snowdonia to collect Winifred's remains.

But who was St Winifred? Why should she fit the bill so perfectly?

Winifred, as happens in all the best stories, was a stunningly beautiful maiden. However, she rejected the possible joys of marriage in favour of living a quiet life serving God. One day, when she was alone and unattended, a man turned up at her home intent on ravishing her. Terrified, Winifred fled down the hillside towards the nearby village but the man chased after her. Desperate to stop her reaching the village and telling the locals what he had tried to do, when he caught up with her he drew his sword and sliced off her head. Then he ran. (Some versions have it that the killer was a man named Prince Cradocus, and that he killed her because she refused to give in.)

Winifred was fortunate in that, just as she was attacked, the village priest, St Bueno (also her brother, in some accounts), came out of his church and saw what had happened. Reaching the young girl, he picked her head up off the ground and replaced it on her shoulders.

Above   *St Winifred – note the bandage around her neck.*

Left   *All that remains of St Winifred's medieval shrine.*

## SHREWSBURY ABBEY

—❧—

Roger de Montgomery was inspired to found Shrewsbury Abbey by one of his clerks, a man called Odelirius. Odelirius had travelled through Europe and been most impressed by some of the monastic houses he had seen, and so he suggested to Roger that he should establish just such a centre in the territories that he had just been given by William I.

The story goes that Roger looked at all the churches already in the town of Shrewsbury and selected a little wooden church sitting by the bank of the River Severn. Roger entered the church, laid his gloves on the altar and dedicated the church as an abbey. A year later, in 1084, Roger became a monk in the abbey he had founded. Cynics might say that, having been a warrior all his life and killed goodness knows how many, Roger was ensuring that he would be accepted in Heaven after his death. Whatever the reasons behind his decision, when he died Roger was buried in Shrewsbury Abbey and his (much later) tomb can still be found there.

As happened with so many of the men who came over with William the Conqueror, on his death Roger's lands were divided between his sons. The elder son inherited his territories in France whilst Hugh, the younger son, got the English lands. Hugh was to die fourteen years later, in 1098, when he was fighting a group of Viking raiders in Anglesey led by Magnus Barefoot, the King of Norway. It is said that Hugh was so well covered by his armour that no part of him was exposed. However, he was killed when he was struck in the eye by an arrow and pitched into the sea. He probably drowned.

On Hugh's death Robert, the older of Roger's sons, acquired the English lands, along with those in France that he already held. Robert de Belleme was a particularly nasty character. It is said that on one occasion he let around 300 of his prisoners starve to death. His reason? Well, it was Lent, and so the prisoners would have had smaller rations than normal anyway – which, in this case, meant no food at all.

—❧—

Miraculously, according to the legend, Winifred came back to life again.

She was a perfect candidate for sainthood. She spent the rest of her days living quietly in Gwytherin in Snowdonia; 450 years later, the monks from Shrewsbury Abbey turned up to collect her bones and take them to Shrewsbury.

Meanwhile, at the spot where, for a few moments, her head had rested, a spring suddenly sprang up. That spring still exists – today it is the well at Holywell in northern Wales that gives the town its name. To this day it is considered one of the most holy places of pilgrimage in the country. Looking into the waters, you can see that some of the stones in the well look red in colour. They still, according to the tale, carry stains from the blood of the saint.

Ellis Peters' *A Morbid Taste for Bones* has the story of St Winifred and the translation of her bones from Wales to Shrewsbury as its background. Although written as a single book, it was to become the first in a series of twenty novels about Brother Cadfael, a monk detective in an age before DNA or even fingerprints.

# EXECUTED ON THE ORDERS OF THE KING!

**K**ING HENRY I had a slight problem. Although he had many children, only two of them were legitimate. Henry's problem was compounded in November 1120 when his only legitimate son was drowned when the ship he was travelling on (*La Blanche-Nef* or *White Ship*) sank in the English Channel. This left Henry with only one legitimate child – a daughter, Matilda. He did his best to ensure that, on his death, Matilda would succeed him. He insisted that all the lords, earls, barons, wealthy merchants and anyone else of importance in the land should swear allegiance to Matilda. Then he died, believing that all would be well.

But it wasn't to be.

Matilda's cousin, Stephen, stole her throne. It wasn't as though Stephen had no claim to the throne: like Matilda, he was a grandchild of William the Conqueror. Many believed that Stephen's claim to the throne was just as good as Matilda's – or, indeed, even better, as he was also a man. Whatever the rights of it, Stephen arrived in England and raced up to Winchester, where he grabbed control of England's Treasury. From there he went to Canterbury and got himself crowned by the Archbishop. This left all those lords, earls, barons etc. in a bit of a quandary. Who should they support? Did they break their sworn oath to Matilda? Or should they go against a King, now anointed in the sight of God?

Consequently, for much of Stephen's reign, all the powerful lords in the land tended to sit safely on fences, coming off them only to snatch what lands they could from each other in the uncertain times that prevailed. It got to be so bad that one of the chroniclers of the day described it as a time when 'God and all his saints slept'. Anarchy ruled.

Stephen, meanwhile, as King, had to go around individual towns and cities asserting his authority. He arrived at Shrewsbury to find the gates closed to him and the castle being held by one of Matilda's staunch supporters, Walter FitzAlan, and so he laid siege to the castle. The English language is a wonderful thing. The word *besiege* comes from the French word, *siege*, meaning seat – because when an army besieges a castle it can sit around for weeks, months or even years, just waiting...

## DROWNINGS ON THE *WHITE SHIP*

When the *White Ship* sank in November 1120, only one person on board survived. Those lost included many of the highest of the land. King Henry I lost another of his sons, an illegitimate one this time, Richard; others who drowned included the Earl and Countess of Chester, the archdeacon of Hereford and a niece of the King. Stephen had originally intended to travel on the *White Ship* too, but at the last moment had changed his mind. Some say that this was due to his concern that the ship appeared to be overcrowded; others say that he didn't feel well, as he was suffering at the time from diarrhoea...

Finally, after about three weeks, the castle surrendered. Intent on capturing Walter FitzAlan, Stephen entered the castle – only to find that his quarry had flown. Walter had escaped through a postern gate in the castle walls and was presumed to have fled into Wales. (He was later to be found in Scotland, where he became High Steward for Matilda's uncle, King David. There he founded a dynasty of Stewards – or Stuarts, as they became known – who were eventually to rule both Scotland and England.)

Back in Shrewsbury, Stephen, discovering that he had missed a fine opportunity to capture one of Matilda's main supporters, lost his temper. Furious, he ordered that the entire garrison of the castle should be executed 'for their obstinacy'.

No one knows for certain how many men were strung up and hanged from the castle walls. Some say there were around sixty; others estimate that it was nearer ninety. The number, however, is irrelevant – it's the deed that counts. This is, without a doubt, the bloodiest event in the history of Shrewsbury Castle.

But it didn't end there. Executing all those common soldiers did Stephen's own reputation no good at all. Nobody at the time would have raised so much as an eyebrow had Stephen executed Walter had he captured him. Walter, as leader, could be held to be responsible; his men, on the other hand, were merely following orders. Stephen's execution of the entire garrison could not, therefore, be justified and he lost a great deal of respect as a result. He was never to make such a precipitous move again.

## HISTORY OF THE CASTLE

The castle was also the innovation of Roger de Montgomery. When, soon after the Norman Conquest, he arrived in Scrobbesbyrig, he found a thriving settlement with a population of belligerent Saxons, any one of whom would have been happy to lead

*Shrewsbury Castle in the 1920s.*

a rebellion against Roger and his men. Suppression of any such possibility was necessary and so, to show his authority and power, Roger immediately ordered the building of a castle. The first castle was a wooden motte-and-bailey castle and, in order to build it, over fifty houses in the town were destroyed – hardly a move likely to promote good relations with the townspeople, but I don't suppose Roger cared much for that.

Within fifty years that wooden castle had been replaced by a stone structure and, besides controlling the recently-conquered English, it also served as one of a whole stream of castles protecting the length of the English/Welsh border. Its importance as a border castle could be said to have lasted almost until the unification of England and Wales under Henry VII, in 1485, when its military role was abandoned.

By Elizabethan times it had become a private house (although, with the outbreak of the Civil War in the 1640s, it was briefly, if ineffectively, refortified).

Then, towards the end of the eighteenth century, it came into the hands of Sir William Pulteney, MP for Shrewsbury. Sir William was said by some to be the richest commoner in England at the time and so, when he decided to convert the former castle into a home, no expense was spared. He employed Thomas Telford to do the job and Telford inserted new floor levels here and cut new doors and windows there, thus turning the building into a very upmarket family home. It was Telford who also built Laura's Tower on the top of the early motte. Laura, incidentally, was Pulteney's daughter and this delightful gazebo was a coming-of-age present for her.

With the twentieth century came a new purpose for the building: it was bought in 1924 by the Shropshire Horticultural Society and presented to

21

the town of Shrewsbury, and then used as the town's Council Chamber. Inevitably the Council outgrew the premises and so, since 1985, it has been the home of the Shropshire Regimental Museum.

Interestingly, the castle was attacked as recently as 1992. This last attack in its history was a bomb planted by the IRA – as a military museum, the castle was deemed to be a legitimate target. There was considerable damage, particularly as a result of smoke, and so a major overhaul of the building and its contents, including the general presentation of all the artefacts, then followed. The Castle Museum reopened in 1995.

The castle also houses the collection of the Shropshire Regimental Museum. Over the years various Shropshire regiments have been formed, then disbanded, then reformed in a slightly different format, disbanded once again... and so it goes on. Consequently, many different wars and campaigns feature in the museum.

One regiment remembered here was the 85th Light Infantry, who fought in the war of 1812 in the United States. This 'army of the Potomac' attacked the city of Washington and burned down the original White House in August 1814.

## BLOUDIE JACK, THE BLUEBEARD OF SHREWSBURY CASTLE

One legend of Shrewsbury Castle is particularly famous: that of Bloudie Jack. He is thought to have been a soldier living at the castle sometime in the eleventh century. He must have been a good-looking and charming man if he did exist, as he seems to have had no problems whatsoever enticing young girls into his arms. With promises of marriage they willingly went with him, secretly, to the castle.

Once in the castle, however, Bloudie Jack's true nature was revealed. Here he had his evil way with the girls and then, to ensure that no one ever discovered just what he had been up to, he would murder the girls and dispose of their bodies some distance from the castle. But each time he killed one of his victims Bloudie Jack kept a souvenir – he would chop off the fingers of the girl and hide them in a chest.

Several girls disappeared in Shrewsbury and nobody had any idea what could have happened to them. None of the girls had given so much as a hint that they even had a lover whom they might have gone off with. Searches were made, but the girls were never found.

Finally, one girl disappeared who had been so excited by her romance with Bloudie Jack that she had revealed their relationship to her sister. When she subsequently disappeared her sister was suspicious and, choosing a time when the castle was empty, she carried out a search. She found the gruesome evidence – the fingers of at least eight girls – hidden away in Jack's chest. The alarm was raised and Bloudie Jack was arrested, tried and found guilty of the murder of all the girls who had disappeared.

Bloody Jack, as he is now usually known to Shrewsbury people, was executed at the top of Pride Hill. It is said, as he stood on the scaffold with the baying crowd all around, that he cursed them all.

## ONE CORPSE TOO MANY

If you've read any of the Brother Cadfael novels written by Ellis Peters, you will probably be under the impression that Shrewsbury was the murder capital of twelfth-century England. The second book in the series was set at the time of the siege of Shrewsbury Castle by King Stephen, and tells how a murder was committed while, up at the castle, so many official murders were also being carried out. Having been ordered to prepare the bodies for burial, Brother Cadfael does what no one expects and counts them – only to discover there is *One Corpse Too Many* (the title of the book). He then sets outs to find the murderer.

Only a few years later, soldiers in the 66th Regiment of Foot found themselves in St Helena guarding Napoleon Bonaparte; Napoleon referred to his Shropshire guards as his 'Red Regiment'. One of the officers, Captain Poppleton, was assigned to Napoleon as his aide-de-camp and it was to Poppleton that Napoleon later gave the lock of his hair that is to be found in the museum.

Perhaps the grandest treasure in the museum, however, is Grand-Admiral Karl Dönitz's baton. Dönitz had first made a name for himself serving in U-boats in the First World War. By the time the Second World War broke out he was in command of the German U-boat fleet and

later, in 1943, he became commander-in-chief of the German Navy. He was chosen as Hitler's successor as leader of the Third Reich and so, when Hitler committed suicide in April 1945, Dönitz became Fuhrer. This was a post that he was to hold for less than a month until, on 23 May 1945, he surrendered to Major General Churcher, commanding the 159th Infantry Brigade in Flensburg.

When he surrendered, Dönitz presented Churcher with his baton. It is particularly fine, decorated as it is with platinum, gold and silver. The baton had been presented to Dönitz by Adolf Hitler in 1943 and was a symbol of his high ranking.

# AD 1283

# PRINCE DAFYDD OF WALES

## Hanged, Drawn and Quartered

**I**T ALL STARTED in Dark Age times when an early Saxon King defeated a Welsh Prince in battle. Following his victory the Saxon King insisted that the Welsh Prince should swear fealty to him and recognise him as his overlord. There was no going back for the other Welsh Princes once this had happened. From then on, no King of England was prepared to consider a Welsh Prince as anything other than a vassal. Consequently, any Welsh rebellions or incursions against the English were seen as traitorous.

Dafydd ap Gruffydd (1238-1283), or 'David of Griffith', was one such Welsh Prince. At the age of four, he was sent to the English court of Henry III as a hostage to ensure his father's good behaviour. However, Dafydd's loyalty to the English throne was to be short-lived. In March 1282, now a man, he began a revolt against King Edward I by attacking Hawarden Castle. Dafydd captured the castle and its constable, Roger Clifford, was killed. The revolt spread throughout northern and central Wales. Llywelyn, Dafydd's brother, was captured and killed the following December, so Dafydd

assumed the title of Prince of Wales. His rebellion, and his time as Prince of Wales, was to be tragically short-lived.

With their far superior forces the English army soon routed the Welsh, forcing Dafydd to seek refuge in the mountains of Snowdonia – from where he was eventually betrayed and captured by the English. He was taken first to Chester and then on to Shrewsbury, where King Edward I called a Parliament in order to decide what should be done with him.

In the Chapter House of Shrewsbury Abbey, Prince Dafydd was tried for treason, for the murder of Roger Clifford, the constable of Hawarden Castle, for sacrilege (Clifford's murder having taken place over the Easter period), and for further plotting against his King and overlord. It was a foregone conclusion that he should be found guilty.

On 30 September Prince Dafydd was condemned to death. Three days later he was the first prominent person to suffer the ignominious execution of hanging, drawing and quartering. Attached to a horse's tail, he was dragged from Shrewsbury Abbey up the hill and

*Hawarden, attacked by Dafydd as his first act of rebellion.*

through the town to the top of Pride Hill, where his execution took place in a crowded open market place.

This particularly sadistic form of punishment was invented in 1241 to execute a pirate called William Maurice. It has long been the rule in English law that different punishments could be handed down for different elements of a single crime. So, if a man broke into a house he would receive a punishment for that. If, in the course of this crime, he stole some silver, attacked the daughter of the household and then wounded the householder as he made his getaway, punishments would be meted out for each separate crime. These days this element in the law still runs true, but such individual punishments are generally given as separate terms of imprisonment running concurrently.

Similarly, in the years that followed its invention, the hanging, drawing and quartering elements of the punishment came to be codified within English law as suitable punishments for different crimes. Prince Dafydd was first dragged from Shrewsbury Abbey (where he had received his sentence) to the site of his execution. He would have been dragged backwards to show that his crime was unnatural. He was thus shown to all the townspeople 'as a traitor to the King who (had) made him a Knight' before being hanged for his 'murder of the gentleman taken in the Castle of Hawarden'. Hanging took place 'between heaven and earth' to show that the victim was unworthy of both. Prince Dafydd's innards were then removed and burnt in front of him because 'he had profaned by assassination the solemnity of Christ's passion'.

A man's 'privy parts' were often also cut off and burned in front of him – this was to signify that he was unfit either to 'be begotten or beget'. If the traitor was a woman, however, she

25

NEAR THIS SPOT
DAVID III PRINCE OF WALES
WAS EXECUTED 3RD. OCTOBER 1283
HE WAS TRIED FOR HIGH TREASON
BY THE PARLIAMENT WHICH MET AT
SHREWSBURY 30TH. SEPTEMBER 1283
AND WAS SENTENCED TO BE HANGED,
DRAWN, BEHEADED, AND QUARTERED.
THIS WAS THE FIRST PARLIAMENT IN WHICH
THE COMMONS WERE REPRESENTED.
LONDON AND 20 OTHER CITIES AND
BOROUGHS (INCLUDING SHREWSBURY)
EACH RETURNED TWO BURGESSES.

THE CROSS AT THIS ROAD JUNCTION WAS
PRESENTED TO THE CORPORATION OF
SHREWSBURY BY SHREWSBURY SCHOOL TO
MARK THE OCCASION OF THE SCHOOL'S
FOURTH CENTENARY AND THE GOODWILL
EXISTING BETWEEN THE SCHOOL AND
THE TOWN.
IT STANDS ON THE SPOT WHERE, UNTIL
1705, THE HIGH CROSS STOOD AND WAS
FORMALLY HANDED OVER TO THE TOWN
BY THE CHAIRMAN OF THE GOVERNING
BODY OF SHREWSBURY SCHOOL
(SIR OFFLEY WAKEMAN BARONET)
AND RECEIVED BY THE MAYOR
(ALDERMAN J. M. WEST) ON 19TH JUNE 1952
IN THE PRESENCE OF THE HEADMASTER
(J. M. PETERSON ESQ.) THE SCHOOL AND
THE TOWN COUNCIL.
MUNICIPIO DILECTO REGIA SCHOLA
SALOPIENSIS SEDE NON FIDE MUTATA

NEAR THIS PLACE
THE EARL OF WORCESTER,
SIR RICHARD VENABLES
AND SIR RICHARD VERNON
WERE EXECUTED ON
MONDAY 23RD JULY 1403
AFTER THE BATTLE OF SHREWSBURY
(FOUGHT ON THE 21ST.)
AND THE DEAD BODY OF
HARRY PERCY (HOTSPUR)
WAS HERE PLACED BETWEEN
TWO MILL STONES AND AFTERWARDS
BEHEADED AND QUARTERED.

was burnt instead – it would have been considered improper to expose her private parts. This was the sentence given to Alice de Lisle in 1685, mentioned later in this book.

Prince Dafydd's final punishment was to be beheaded. His quarters were then displayed in those different parts of the country where he had 'compassed the death of his lord the king'. Afterwards his head was sent to join that of his brother, Llewelyn, on a spike over one of the gates to the Tower of London. His executioner, Geoffrey of Shrewsbury, was paid twenty shillings for carrying out the task.

The last such execution was carried out in 1782, although hangings and beheadings went on for considerably longer. It was nearly 100 years before the sentence of hanging, drawing and quartering was formally abolished in 1867. In the meantime, others who suffered this end included William Wallace (the Scottish rebel), a number of Catholic martyrs, and Guy Fawkes and his fellow conspirators of the Gunpowder Plot.

## WALLS AGAINST THE WELSH

So far as the people of Shropshire were concerned, those Welsh were a troublesome race. They were always coming across the border to cause mayhem, steal a few head of cattle or capture a castle and hold its inmates to ransom. This had happened since before anyone could remember and, all along the border, Englishmen were forever on the lookout for raiding parties. (Shrewsbury's very name tells us that it was a fortified town from Saxon times – the *bury* element in a Saxon place name indicates this.)

Sure enough, Shrewsbury was regularly attacked. The Welsh would steal into the town, hold its merchants to ransom, rape their daughters, collect a few souvenirs to take home and then, having shown those English that they could take the town any time they wished, they would depart ... until the next time. The castle itself may have been well protected, but as for the town ... whatever type of fortifications the early town had to protect itself with were obviously not good enough. It is probable that they consisted merely of some form of rampart with or without a palisade on the top.

Eventually, in the 1240s, King Henry III decided that enough was enough and decreed that proper stone walls should be built all around the town. These town walls survive in many parts of the town, one street following the wall known as Town Walls.

But there's no need to go to the medieval town boundary to see the old wall. Pop into McDonald's in Pride Hill, wander downstairs and there it is. Interestingly, one would think that in a town like Shrewsbury, where the walls were required for defence, access would be needed all along a wall's length by anyone wanting to protect the town.

But it would appear that no sooner had the walls been completed then the townspeople felt completely secure from attack – so much so that they almost immediately began to build their houses abutting directly onto the wall. This is what has happened in McDonald's, where large windows have been cut into the wall. Built into the wall in McDonald's is what appears to be a tiny little room – it's furnished these days with a small table and, because of its low ceiling, is very popular with young children as a place in which to sit and eat their burgers. In fact, it's an old *garderobe* or toilet – the word comes from the French *garder* (meaning to protect) and *robe* (meaning clothes). Apparently, in medieval times wealthy people who had more than one change of clothes would often keep their spare clothes in the

*Town walls behind McDonald's. This image shows how the medieval town walls have been subsumed by later buildings, right up to modern times, but have not quite been lost.*

vicinity of a privy because the smell of ammonia in the urine would keep moths away. I hate to think what people smelt like when they all dressed in their best for special events...

## THE FIRST TRUE PARLIAMENT

When Prince Dafydd was tried for treason, King Edward I was determined that his trial would appear to be totally above-board and fair (despite the fact that he had probably already decided on its outcome). Consequently, he called a Parliament so that the Prince would be seen to be tried by his peers.

In those days Parliaments were called by the King in order to confirm laws and taxes. They were not the governing bodies that we know today. This particular Parliament included men from the lords, the Church and the laity; this last consisted of representatives of the various boroughs around the country, usually the more wealthy merchants.

The Parliament called by King Edward to try Prince Dafydd was held in the Chapter House of Shrewsbury Abbey. Once the trial had come to an end its business was completed – so far as the King was concerned.

The merchants, however, had other ideas. They decided to adjourn the Parliament and moved to nearby Acton Burnell, home of Robert Burnell, Bishop of Bath and Wells, friend and adviser to the King and Chancellor of England. Here they reopened the Parliament, sitting in the Great Barn, the gable ends of which still sit in grounds next to the castle. In the course of their deliberations they passed a law stipulating that all

*Remains of the Great Barn, site of the first Parliament called by the Commons rather than the King.*

## ENGLISH PRINCES OF WALES

Dafydd was the last Welsh Prince of Wales. His death left a vacuum which, sooner or later, would have been filled by some other Welsh contender for the title. This was the last thing that King Edward I wanted.

Soon after Dafydd's execution, King Edward was in Caernarvon and realised that he could use this vacuum to his own advantage. Calling all the nobles of Wales to his Court, he asked them who should become Prince of Wales. The Welsh, naturally, had no wish to see any English protégé of the King's being given the title and were naturally suspicious. King Edward told them that he had found the ideal person for the position – a Prince of royal blood who had been born in Wales and who, moreover, spoke not a word of English. Couldn't be better, thought the Welsh, and promptly agreed that this Prince should succeed to the title.

What the Welsh nobles were unaware of was that King Edward's wife had just given birth to a son. Presented with the baby, the men realised that they had been tricked into agreeing. However, they had no option, having given their word, but to accept the new Prince. Ever since that time, the first-born son of an English monarch has been given the title 'Prince of Wales'.

---

debtors, when they borrowed money, had to agree a date by which the debt should be repaid. This was a novel idea in an age when repayment of a debt would usually be drawn out interminably, often until the debtor died – at which point his heirs would refuse to have anything to do with it.

The Act is known as the 'Statute of Acton Burnell' and its importance lies not so much in the Act itself but rather in the fact that it was codified at a Parliament that had been called by the members of the House of Commons, rather than by the King – the first time this had ever happened.

# AD 1403

# THE BATTLE OF SHREWSBURY

## THE MAIN PROTAGONISTS

### King Henry IV

Henry IV (1367-1413), known as Henry of Bolinbroke, was the cousin of King Richard II. Both men were the grandsons of Edward III.

Richard exiled Henry after a quarrel. While Henry was away, his father died; Richard then seized all the family's property. This was too much for Henry, who immediately returned to England. He landed in Yorkshire, where he declared that he had no pretensions to the throne. He signed an oath, now known as the 'Doncaster Declaration', in which he said that he was merely intent on reclaiming what was rightfully his. People of all ranks flocked to Henry's support – after all, if King Richard could steal his own cousin's inheritance, who in the land was safe from such a theft? Amongst Henry's many supporters was the powerful Percy family of Northumberland.

Before long, Henry forced Richard to abdicate and proclaimed himself King. Richard disappears from history at this point. It's generally accepted that he was imprisoned in Pontefract Castle, where he was deliberately starved to death. But no one knows for sure. Some say that he was taken to Scotland and done away with there, out of the country. Whatever happened to him, there can be no doubt that his disappearance and subsequent death would have been arranged on the orders of King Henry.

Not a particularly pleasant character, it wasn't long before King Henry IV began to make himself unpopular. He raised taxes, interfered in Parliament, and started to argue with his former supporters.

### Sir Henry Percy

When he wrote *Henry IV Part I*, which dealt with the events surrounding the Battle of Shrewsbury, William Shakespeare 'did a Hollywood' – in other words he changed many of the facts to suit the story that he wanted to tell.

One of the most easily verifiable facts that Shakespeare changed was the age of Sir Henry Percy. In the play, Percy is depicted as being a contemporary of the

Left *Henry IV at his coronation.*

Right *Henry IV's statue stands guard over the battlefield from the east end of Battlefield church.*

King's son, the sixteen-year-old Prince Henry. Sir Henry Percy was actually a contemporary of King Henry. The two men would have known each other well from boyhood and, in fact, they had both been knighted in the same ceremony when aged around eleven.

Sir Henry Percy was the eldest son of the Earl of Northumberland. His family had ruled vast swathes of north-eastern England for generations, guarding English interests along the Scottish borderlands. They were warriors through and through and Harry Hotspur, as he is more often known, was true to the breed. He had fought in his first battle when still only fourteen and grew up to be considered the finest and most highly respected soldier in all of Christendom. His nickname, incidentally, was given to him by the Scots because of the hot-headed way in which he would spur his horse into the thick of any fighting.

By the time of the Battle of Shrewsbury, Hotspur had been fighting

for England's cause for years, first under King Richard and then King Henry. He had carried out regular campaigns not only into Scotland but also along the northern English/Welsh borders, going deep into Wales from Chester, where he was based. Campaigns cost money – wages for soldiers, armaments, food – and the money to pay for these campaigns came out of the Percy strongbox. There are numerous records in the archives of the time of letters going from Hotspur to Henry IV asking for help in financing the campaigns and of letters from Henry to Hotspur promising that such financial help would be forthcoming. It never was.

Then, in 1402, Hotspur won a victory in Scotland – the Battle of Homildon Hill. As a result Hotspur captured several Scottish knights, the ransoming of whom would go a long way towards covering his expenses. And then Henry IV insisted that the captured knights should be passed on to him so that he could claim the ransom. (It should be

*The arms of the protagonists: Black Douglas, Sir Richard Sandford, Sir Peter de Dutton, Sir Robert Goushill and Harry Hotspur.*

pointed out that this was very much against the code of practice of the day. True, when ransoms were paid the King would always get his cut, but it was not up to the King to take the lot and then decide whether or not to share it amongst those who had taken the prisoner in the first place, many of whom would have been very low down the social scale and unlikely to be paid by the King in such circumstances.)

This was too much for Hotspur – and when he heard that the King was not only referring to him as a traitor but also planning to march to Northumberland with an army, he decided to rebel.

## Black Douglas

Archibald Douglas, the 4th Earl of Douglas, was one of the Scottish knights captured at the Battle of Homildon Hill the previous year. Refusing to be handed over to King Henry, Douglas and his fellow Scots were released by Hotspur when he decided upon rebellion. Douglas, feeling that it would be the chivalric thing to do, decided to join with Hotspur at Shrewsbury:

> Archibald, earl of Douglas, wreaked so much slaughter that besides others he killed with his great mace three men disguised as kings in the hope that each was the real King Henry, inasmuch as

they were wearing surcoats with coats of arms and royal coronets on top of their helmets...

In the course of the battle Black Douglas, as he was known, suffered a severe wound – one of his testicles was sliced off. Tradition has it that he attempted to escape the battlefield by riding a horse but, perhaps not surprisingly, he soon came a cropper and was captured once again, this time by Henry's forces. In due course he returned to his estates in Scotland and eventually died in the Battle of Verneuil in France in 1424. He was buried in Tours Cathedral.

## Sir Richard Sandford

Sir Richard Sandford, fighting for the King's forces, received his knighthood on the morning of the battle. He was killed that same day.

Coincidences are strange things. Six hundred years later, in 2003, the Mayor of Shrewsbury leading the celebrations for the anniversary of the battle was Mrs Eileen Sandford – the wife of a direct descendent of Sir Richard.

## Sir Peter Dutton

You may have received the impression from reading the above accounts of the battle that the author is very much on the side of the rebel Harry Hotspur

## WHY SHROPSHIRE?

If Hotspur was in Northumberland when he decided to rebel and King Henry was then in London, why on earth was the battle fought in Shropshire? There are several reasons for this.

For one thing, Hotspur knew he could raise an army quickly in Cheshire, where the local people were always on the alert for trouble in Wales. Hotspur also hoped to meet up with the Welsh leader, Owen Glendower, although this never came to pass.

Then there was a third reason – for a couple of years King Henry's eldest son and heir, Prince Henry (or Hal, as Shakespeare calls him), had been based in Shrewsbury Castle undergoing military training. If he could capture the young Prince, Hotspur knew that he would have the ultimate bargaining tool in any discussions with the King. Both men raced with their armies to Shrewsbury and, unfortunately, King Henry got their first, with only hours to spare.

And so the battle was fought the following day, just outside the town.

---

in this battle. You would be correct. Consequently it was with great delight when, on researching my family tree, I discovered that one of my ancestors not only fought at the battle but fought with Hotspur. Sir Peter Dutton was one of many Cheshire knights on the losing side and was lucky to survive with his head intact afterwards. Dutton was given a 'general pardon... for all the offences committed by him whilst in rebellion with Henry Percy the son, and other rebels'. Mind you, he and the other Cheshire lords (which included members of the powerful Grosvenor, Massey and Legh families, amongst others) had to pay considerable amounts of money for the privilege.

### Sir Robert Goushill

Like Richard Sandford, Robert Goushill was knighted by King Henry IV on the morning of the Battle of Shrewsbury. He was subsequently wounded in the battle but managed to crawl to relative safety under a hedge, where one of his servants later found him. The servant asked how he fared and Sir Robert told him that he was almost suffocating under the weight of his armour.

Once his armour had been removed Sir Robert, fearing that he might still die, told the servant where he had hidden a casket with sixty marks in it and asked the servant to retrieve it and take it to his wife. The temptation was too much for the servant and he drove a dagger into his lord's heart, holding it there until the quivering body was stilled. Then he removed from the corpse all jewels, rings and marks of identification and made off.

But the servant had been seen by a wounded squire who had also sought refuge under the hedge. This squire, when he was later brought in from the battlefield, raised the alarm and a search was made for the servant. Found with all his plunder, the murdering servant was later hanged.

## THE BATTLE

On 21 July 1403, two armies faced each other across some fields to the north of the town of Shrewsbury. They were quite evenly matched; it's thought today that the King's army numbered between 12,000 and 14,000 men whilst Hotspur's army was around 10,000 to 12,000. Each army included 3,000 longbow archers.

They faced each other for most of the day whilst, in no-man's land between, parleys took place. These failed, and at around four o'clock that afternoon battle was joined when the King's archers moved within range of Hotspur's army and the archers from both armies let fly with their arrows.

According to chroniclers of the day, 'the sky turned black with arrows' and 'men fell like apples in an orchard in autumn'. It must have been horrendous.

Having used up their arrows, the two armies converged. Hand-to-hand fighting broke out – no quarter was given. Unlike battles at Homildon Hill or in France at the period, there was no reason to capture people for possible ransom. It was kill or be killed. In an age when ferocity was expected in battle, the ferocity shown by soldiers on both sides at Shrewsbury appalled everyone.

The King had several decoys on the battlefield, dressed in the same armour. At one point in the battle one of the King's look-alikes fell. Seeing this, his forces started to waver. There was panic and some began to fall back, looking for a retreat. Hotspur rapidly took advantage of the situation, pushing his own men forward.

Meantime, the left flank of the King's army was being led by his sixteen-year-old son, Prince Henry, who led his forces into the fray, attacking Hotspur's flank. In all probability this manoeuvre on the part of the Prince slowed down Hotspur's advance, giving the King's men time to regroup.

The entire battle lasted for around three hours and, for all the fighting amongst individuals on the field, the outcome was entirely dependent on which of the two protagonists fell first. It so happened that it was Harry

*General view of the battlefield, showing the church to the right and, in the distance, the ridge where Harry Hotspur's army faced the King.*

*The death of Harry Hotspur.*

Hotspur who was killed. Even the most experienced soldier on the field, which Hotspur undoubtedly was, has at some point to raise his visor, if only to get a breath of air. It must have been when Hotspur paused to do just this that some marksman shot him, the arrow piercing his throat and going through his jugular vein, killing him instantly.

The battle was over. Hotspur's men began to run for their lives, many of them being chased and cut down even as they fled.

## WEAPONS, WOUNDS AND BODIES

There was somewhere between 22,000 and 26,000 men on the field, fighting in a battle that lasted for some three hours. By the end of that time it is considered a conservative estimate that 6,000 men were dead or dying – roughly a quarter

of the field. It all goes to emphasise not just the ferocity of the fighting but the effectiveness of the weapons the men used.

The Battle of Shrewsbury may not be important historically (after all, no dynasty changed hands) but it was militarily important. It was the first battle fought on English soil where both sides used the longbow – to devastating effect. The longbow was the Exocet missile of its day.

To use a longbow effectively required training from an early age. Laws were passed insisting that all boys over the age of seven should start regular archery practice, and that no archer over the age of twenty-four was to shoot at a target of less that 220 yards distance. At one time even the playing of football on a Sunday was banned, because it would interfere with practice at the archery butts.

But training men in this way could prove to be extremely risky – you were to all intents and purposes training potential killing machines, and this only twenty years after the Peasants' Revolt had shaken the entire country. Indeed, you needed a great deal of faith in your men if you were to use such weapons. In Scotland, for example, clan chieftains didn't have the necessary control over their people to insist on regular training whilst the French, on the other hand, didn't trust their lower orders enough to allow them the use of such a weapon.

Once fully trained, a longbow archer was capable of shooting up to twelve or fifteen arrows a minute. Imagine, therefore, what it must have been like to be under a barrage of arrows being shot at a rate of perhaps ten a minute by 3,000 archers – 30,000 arrows

## NEVER IGNORE A SOOTHSAYER'S WARNING

It is said that on the morning of the battle, Harry Hotspur was donning his armour when he realised that he had left his favourite sword in the village where he had camped the night before. He told his squire to find it. The squire replied:

'Yes, sire, I'll go straight back to Berwick and get it.'

On hearing the name of the village, Hotspur turned white.

'Then has my plough reached its last furrow,' he said, realising that he would die that day. Apparently a soothsayer, many years before, had warned him that he would die 'near Berwick'. Of course, to a lad from Northumberland there was only one Berwick...

Another soothsayer told King Henry where he would die – in Jerusalem. Having been to Jerusalem on a crusade in the 1390s and survived, Henry happily ignored the warning. Where did he die? In the Palace of Westminster, in a room known as the Jerusalem Chamber.

every minute – for five minutes. (The French army, by comparison, employed mercenary Italian crossbowmen but even the fastest of them could only let off two darts in a minute.)

Some archers trained to become marksmen and it is said that such men could, from a distance of 200 yards, shoot an arrow though a man's helmet visor – it was obviously just such an archer who took the lucky shot that killed Hotspur.

In medieval times it was often better to be killed outright on the battlefield than to be wounded. If you were wounded (and didn't bleed to death before help arrived) then you would have a surgeon care for you. Surgeons tended to be barbers in peacetime – this is why a barber's pole is white with red stripes, signifying blood-soaked white bandages. Their knives (never clean and often rusty) would be used to dig out arrowheads or splinters and often therefore introduced tetanus, causing gangrene in wounds that, had clean tools been used, people might have recovered from.

The Prince suffered a severe wound, received as he led his men into the attack on Hotspur's flank. An arrow struck him in the cheek. His men told him to retire, but the sixteen-year-old refused. He could hardly continue to fight with the shaft of an arrow sticking out of his face: someone must have broken it off for him. Somehow he fought on, and eventually he passed out – weakened by loss of blood and sheer exhaustion. His unconscious body was taken from the battlefield to Shrewsbury Abbey and then on to Kenilworth Castle, where King Henry's surgeon, John Bradmore, was faced with the task of removing the arrowhead which had lodged itself in Hal's jaw – an impossible task, since arrowheads are deliberately flanged so that they cannot be drawn out backwards without causing further damage.

Fortunately, we know exactly how Bradmore dealt with the injury

*The two armies would have prepared their weapons the night before the battle. It is still possible to see the grooves left when soldiers, camped besides Astley church, sharpened their arrows on the church walls.*

## WHAT HAPPENED TO HOTSPUR'S BODY?

Hotspur's body was recovered and taken north to Whitchurch, where it was buried at St Alkmund's church. The following day rumours started to circulate that he had escaped alive. King Henry therefore ordered his men to retrieve the body from Whitchurch and display it at the top of Pride Hill, in the centre of Shrewsbury. For good measure, the corpse was then executed. In medieval England an execution was as much a public entertainment as anything else – but there's no fun to be had in watching a dead man being executed. And so, to give the crowd something to see, Hotspur's uncle, the Earl of Worcester, and two Cheshire knights, Thomas Venables and Richard Vernon, were executed beside him. It was the full works – hanging, drawing and quartering. At least Hotspur was already dead.

Afterwards the quarters were displayed in various parts of the country. The man charged with arranging this was the Shropshire County Sheriff, Thomas Banaster, whose expense account for first preserving and then transporting the body parts reads as follows:

Four sacks and wax and rosyn for waxing them, cumin, cloves, anice and other spices, and salt put in the sacks to preserve the quarters – 21s 8d.
Four men to carry one quarter to London – £2 13s 4d.
Three men to Bristol – £2.
Four men to Newcastle – £4.
Six men to Chester – £4.
Total cost: £13 15s.

because he wrote up his medical notes afterwards. Somehow he had to pull the arrow out backwards without further mutilating the Prince. He asked a blacksmith to fashion for him a narrow tube that could be inserted into Hal's cheek to isolate the arrow. Then, using tongs, Bradmore gripped the arrow and pulled it out. The 'wounde was wasched with wyne and clensyd' with a mixture that contained honey and, miraculously, the boy recovered. Remember, this was an age before modern antiseptics and penicillin, when even the most basic rules of hygiene would have been ignored. Who knows when Bradmore had last washed his hands, let alone that blacksmith?

Of course, the Prince was left with a hideous scar down his left cheek. If you ever see a portrait of King Henry V, as he later became, you will therefore never see his full face.

## DID YOU KNOW?

The expression 'to keep something under your hat' originally referred to archers keeping their bowstrings safely under their hats in order to keep them dry during wet weather.

One final part of the story took place some months later, when Hotspur's widow was given permission by King Henry to collect all the bits for private burial. This was considered at the time to be extremely forgiving on the part of the King. Interestingly, both York Minster and Beverley Minster claim to be where Hotspur was buried but, in fact, no one knows where he was laid to rest. Hotspur's widow quite deliberately never told anyone where she had had him buried, probably for fear that Henry would change his mind and insist at some later date that he be dug up once again.

## WHAT HAPPENED TO ALL THE OTHER BODIES?

With something in the region of 6,000 bodies to be disposed of after the battle, there remains to this day the mystery of what happened to them. The bodies of knights and anyone of importance would have been recovered and taken for burial elsewhere – there is a particularly fine tomb in St Oswald's church in Ashbourne, Derbyshire, of one such knight, Sir Edmund Cokayne.

But as for the remaining 5,000 or so soldiers... who knows? And who, at the time, really cared? There are many who will tell you that a pit was dug under the site where Battlefield church now stands and the men were buried there. But a pit large enough for that many men? In an age before JCBs?

It is much more probable that many of the bodies were buried in small pits wherever they were found. It's an interesting point that medieval priests would often bless an entire battlefield – this meant that, for the purposes of burial, the whole site could be considered to be consecrated. There was, therefore, no need to carry bodies to one especially consecrated site. In fact, after one battle in France a river was so crammed with bodies that the priests simply consecrated the river and left the bodies to either rot or be washed away.

It's also quite feasible that many of the bodies would have been burnt. This was not generally acceptable religious practice at the time, but these were just the bodies of the common soldiery. Who cared about them? And it would certainly have acted as an excellent fertilizer on what was good agricultural land!

# HENRY TUDOR PASSES THROUGH SHREWSBURY

**S**HREWSBURY IS SAID by many to be the most haunted town in England. One site that is reputed to be the home of a number of ghosts is Barracks Passage.

Most ghosts seem either to haunt the place in which they spent much of their lives or the place where they were killed – this is not the case with the ghosts of Barracks Passage. Here, the ghosts all

## KING HENRY VISITS SHREWSBURY

Henry VII visited Shrewsbury many times after he became King. On one occasion he brought his son and heir, Prince Arthur, with him. Whilst they were in the town they attended a play in a large amphitheatre which was somewhere in the Quarry Gardens, probably where the swimming pool now stands. An absolute fortune was spent by the townspeople on entertaining the King and his court, so perhaps they were quite thankful when Prince Arthur and his new bride, Catherine of Aragon, went to live in Ludlow shortly afterwards...

When, some six months later, Prince Arthur died in Ludlow, his head was buried in St Lawrence's church (although the rest of his body was taken for burial in Worcester). Catherine was subsequently married to Arthur's brother, Henry, and following their divorce she spent a great deal of time in Ludlow with her daughter, the future Queen Mary. Unlike most towns in England, Shrewsbury cannot claim a visit by Queen Elizabeth I. However, at least Bloody Mary is known to have regularly visited.

*Henry VII on a public house sign in Mardol. Though not a pub when the King visited, the building itself was certainly already there.*

Above *Wyle Cop, with the timber-framed Henry Tudor House in the centre.*

Right *Barracks Passage.*

came originally from Wales, and died in Leicestershire. Each spent only a few days, if that, in Shrewsbury.

The Wars of the Roses, as we now call them, were fought over a period of some thirty years between two branches of the royal family – the Yorkists and the Lancastrians. By 1485 it was the Yorkists who were in the ascendant and it was the Yorkist Richard III who was King of England. Both Richard and Henry Tudor, the Lancastrian claimant to the throne, could trace their lineages back to King Edward III – Richard through Edward's fifth son, Edmund, Duke of York, and Henry through Edward's fourth son, John of Gaunt, Duke of Lancaster. However, Henry was descended from an illegitimate son of John of Gaunt (although, by marrying his mistress, John of Gaunt had legitimised the line).

Whatever the rights and wrongs of his claim, Henry raised an army in Wales, marched across the border into England and reached the town of Shrewsbury, where he demanded admittance. This was refused, one of the bailiffs of the town, Thomas Mytton, standing up and announcing that he would only let Henry into the town 'over my belly'. Fearing that Henry's soldiers would then force their way through the town and cause immense damage, the townspeople persuaded Mytton that he had to let Henry in. How could Mytton do so without being seen to go back on his fine words?

Thomas Mytton was obviously a true politician and he got around it very cleverly. He went to the Welsh Bridge to meet Henry, and there he lay down on the ground so that Henry could, literally, step over his belly as he walked across the bridge. Thus Mytton was seen to keep his word.

Once in Shrewsbury, Henry stayed in the building in Wyle Cop that now bears his name. His soldiers presumably found lodgings for themselves throughout the

## THE DEADLY PICTURE

Just across Wyle Cop from Henry Tudor House and Barracks Passage sits a pub, The Nag's Head. The building dates from the early 1400s and has, at the rear, the remains of a medieval hall house that would once have been the home of a wealthy local merchant.

The house became a pub in the 1800s and it offered accommodation for visitors – accommodation with a bit of a risk involved, as it turned out. You took your life – or at least your sanity – in your hands if you stayed in the little room at the top of the house.

In that room, hanging on the wall, was a picture, a painting of a Biblical prophet, and it was said that anyone who looked at the picture would be driven mad. The number of people who have stayed in the room, looked at the picture and come away unscathed is not known. However, there are certainly tales of people who became so crazed when they saw it that they promptly committed suicide. There was a young girl, recently betrothed, who jumped out of the window and was killed when she was run

*The Nag's Head, home of the haunted picture.*

over by a stagecoach that was racing up the street just as she fell. On another occasion a man committed suicide by shooting himself in that room. The painting, incidentally, is still there. But it is now safely locked away in a cupboard...

---

town, but Henry's personal bodyguard were accommodated in the buildings just behind Henry Tudor House, the buildings that now line Barracks Passage – serving as barracks for Henry's men, hence the name. From Shrewsbury Henry and his army marched across England to Leicestershire and there met Richard on Bosworth Field. Battle was joined. Richard was killed, and his crown was conveniently discovered under a hawthorn bush. The crown was

retrieved and placed on Henry's head, thus ushering in the Tudor Age under King Henry VII.

So why do all these ghosts haunt Barracks Passage? We just don't know. But Shrewsbury folk will tell you that their town has a reputation for always giving its visitors a warm welcome. Perhaps those soldiers had such a good time in Shrewsbury that, when they died, they made a deliberate choice to spend the rest of eternity in the town?

# THE BLOODY BISHOP

## The Churchman who Ordered the Hanging of 5,000 Welshmen Dies in Shrewsbury

**W**HATEVER ELSE MAY be said of Bishop Rowland Lee, he can't have been entirely without courage. Imagine how it must have been to be one of King Henry VIII's priests at a time when the King had just broken off all his ties with the Roman Catholic Church and the Pope in Rome.

Whom did you support? The King, of course – that is, if you wanted to keep your head. But, in supporting the King, you had to break with all the religious traditions that you had been taught to uphold and, presumably, to believe. You could support the King easily enough for political expediency but it would be best to try and keep a low profile and do as little as possible to draw attention to yourself or to upset the Church in the meantime – after all, on the Day of Judgement you would have to answer for all your sins, and political expediency would be no excuse.

When Henry VIII broke with Rome and divorced his wife he then wanted to marry Anne Boleyn. The priest who carried out that marriage ceremony certainly had to raise his profile somewhat: a dangerous thing to do in the political climate of the time. Rowland Lee was the priest who carried out that marriage ceremony in 1533.

He was well rewarded, however, becoming Bishop of Lichfield and Coventry the following year. Soon afterwards he also became Lord Lieutenant of the Council in the Marches. This was a post that was directly answerable only to the monarch and so it came with a great deal of individual power.

Following the Battle of Bosworth Field in 1485 Welsh territories had been linked with England. Wales was lawless territory, far too distant to be controlled easily from Westminster. It had therefore been decided that the Principality would be controlled from Ludlow. A Council in the Marches was set up in Ludlow for this purpose and, in 1534, Bishop Lee was put in charge of it.

Lee set to the difficult task of controlling the Welsh with a great deal of fervour. He was not afraid to bring swift and terrifying justice to anyone caught guilty of even the most minor misdemeanour. Within next to no time he had garnered a reputation as 'the

*Bishop Lee's memorial on the walls of Old St Chad's church.*

boasted that he also ordered the hanging of 'five of the best blood of the county of Shropshire as well'.

In 1543, whilst travelling from Ludlow to Chester (the diocese of Lichfield in those days also included the county of Cheshire), he fell ill in Shrewsbury and died in the town, at the college (the home of his brother Sir George Lee, the dean of St Chad's). He was buried in Old St Chad's church.

hanging bishop', and for years after his reign of terror naughty children would be made to behave with threats that 'Rowland Lee will come and get you'.

Apparently, Bishop Lee strongly believed that it was wiser to hang 100 people too many rather than one person too few. On one occasion one of his victims died before he was due to be hanged: Lee was so angry with the man that he ordered that his dead body should be strung up just the same.

All in all, in his nine-year reign of terror, it is said that he ordered the hanging of 5,000 people. And not just Welshmen either. The local Shropshire gentry didn't try to hide their dislike of the man, and Lee wasn't averse to revenging himself on them when the opportunity arose. He is said to have

## PUNISHMENTS

Every town and village in the country was legally required to have a set of stocks ready for the punishment of any miscreants.

Most towns and villages with a suitable pond would also have had a ducking stool, although where there wasn't a pond people were just as likely to be ducked in a river or open sewer. Shrewsbury's ducking stool was over a pond that then could be found in the region of the Square, roughly where Robert Clive stands watch nowadays.

Ducking stools were not just used for nagging wives and prostitutes, as seems to be the prevailing thought these days. Cheating tradesmen were just as likely to get a ducking. Each miscreant would be sentenced to be ducked a certain number of times. Sometimes the sentence would also stipulate how long they should be held under the water, but it was not the intention that people should drown – although many did.

Severe crimes were punishable by hanging. From medieval times theft was considered to be almost as bad as murder and, even to the end of the

## THE COUNCIL IN THE MARCHES

—∞∞∞—

Although founded in 1472 by King Edward IV, it was not until the Tudor period that the Council in the Marches really came into its own.

The Lord President of the Council was in charge of law and order not just throughout Wales but also along the borders: in other words, throughout the counties of Cheshire, Shropshire, Herefordshire, Worcestershire and Gloucestershire. The Council was based in the town of Ludlow and, over the 200 years of its existence, brought a great deal of kudos to the town – which became, in effect, the capital of Wales.

Perhaps the best known Lord President was Sir Henry Sidney (father of Sir Philip Sidney), who was appointed by Queen Elizabeth I in 1560 and served for twenty-six years. The Council was finally abolished in 1689 when Wales's Government moved to London.

—∞∞∞—

1700s, the theft of a sheep or pig would result in the offender being sentenced to be executed in this way, although by this time attitudes were changing. (In fact, there are many Australians today who are descended from sheep stealers whose death sentences were commuted to transportation.)

By the twentieth-century hanging had become a carefully calculated science with the victim weighed beforehand, the drop carefully measured and a decent quality of rope that would not stretch being used, all of which was intended to quicken and – supposedly – lessen the agony of the whole process. But for years beforehand it would have meant a long and drawn-out death, sometimes taking up to an hour before the victim stopped jerking. Indeed, if you had a loved one who had been sentenced to such a death the best thing you could do for them would be to attend the hanging and then, as soon as their body had been hoisted into the air, pull on their legs to hasten death.

Gibbets for such executions were usually on the outskirts of the towns – in Shrewsbury one such place was the area where the Ditherington roundabout now sits. This has given rise to a local joke that people heading for their execution at Ditherington would dither all the way there – actually, they were unlikely to have been given any such opportunity. After the execution had taken place the body would be left hanging until it rotted away. This served as a warning not just to the local people but also to strangers arriving in the town. Occasionally someone would be executed elsewhere and the body then hanged from a gibbet erected solely for the purpose of displaying the body. Gibbets were often shaped like iron cages, thereby ensuring that, as the body disintegrated, all the parts would remain on display. It was in such a cage that Oliver Cromwell's body was displayed at Tyburn in 1661, although he had died some two years before.

# THE HEROIC DEATH OF A FORMER SHREWSBURY SCHOOLBOY

**T**HERE'S A SAYING that 'my enemy's enemy is my friend', and never was this truer than in late sixteenth-century England when the natural enemy of every right-thinking (Protestant) Englishman was Spain. Consequently, anyone who was fighting against the Spanish was considered to be a natural ally with the English.

Today, most people who consider these Spanish wars think in terms of the numerous engagements that took place in the Atlantic Ocean and the seas surrounding the West Indies, where brave English buccaneers strove to steal Spanish gold, itself already stolen from the Aztecs, Incas and other South and Central American peoples. All of this culminated in the defeat in 1588 of the Spanish Armada – a fleet which actually had the effrontery to try and attack England itself.

But this wasn't entirely the case.

For years the Netherlands had been a territory of the Spanish Empire and the country therefore served as a useful base for minor Spanish attacks on England. By the 1580s the Dutch people had begun to fight for independence from

*Sir Philip Sidney.*

the Spanish. Naturally, this was seen as something that deserved English assistance. In 1585, Queen Elizabeth I sent a small army led by Robert Dudley, Earl of Leicester, to fight for the Dutch cause. Amongst the soldiers in that army was Sir Philip Sidney.

Philip Sidney's father, Sir Henry Sidney, as Lord President of the

Council in the Marches, was based in Ludlow and from there had sent his seven-year-old son to be educated in Shrewsbury. Young aristocrats were not usually sent away to school in those days and it's thought that this decision of his father's may have had something to do with the fact that the headmaster at the time, Thomas Ashton, was a sound Protestant. This implies a strong change in Sir Henry's religious beliefs, as the young Philip had been named after his godfather, the Spanish King Philip II, leader of many Roman Catholics throughout Christendom.

After leaving Shrewsbury School, Philip Sidney went on to spend a short while at Oxford University. In the years that followed he became the patron of many of the great poets of the day, including Edmund Spenser. He travelled widely throughout Europe, and became something of an authority on political affairs. He is known to have had interests in law, history and exploration – he nearly joined Sir Francis Drake on his circumnavigation of the world.

He had a natural aptitude as a soldier, serving Queen Elizabeth I on campaign in Ireland and also travelling on diplomatic missions to various parts of Europe. He was in Paris at the time of the St Bartholomew's Day Massacre, where he witnessed atrocities during which thousands of Protestants were killed.

Then, in 1585, he went to Holland. In September of that year the rebellious Dutch found themselves facing their mighty overlords. Even with the help of an English force, which brought their numbers up to around 17,000 men, the Dutch had no chance against a much larger and better-equipped Spanish strength of 25,500 men when they met at the Battle of Zutphen.

During the battle Sir Philip Sidney was one of the foremost soldiers, always in the thick of the fighting. He had one horse killed under him and was in the act of mounting a second horse when he was hit in the thigh by a musket ball. Normally he would have been wearing leg-armour to protect him from just such a chance shot – but, before the battle, he had lent this to a friend.

*Notice that Sir Philip Sidney's statue shows him without his cuisses (thigh armour), recalling the fact that, before the battle, he had lent them to a friend.*

*Battle of Zutphen, where Sidney received his fatal wound.*

The wound was serious and caused him a substantial loss of blood – yet, weak though he was, he still managed to ride a mile back to his camp. Arriving, his squire came to help him from his horse and offered him some water to drink. Looking around, Sidney noticed other wounded soldiers who had made it to the relative safety of the camp. One of them, dying from his wounds, was watching the squire as he offered the bottle to Sidney, obviously longing for a drink himself.

'Give the drink to that soldier,' Sidney said, indicating the dying man. 'His need is greater than mine.'

From the camp Sidney was taken to Arnhem, where it was expected that time would heal his wound and he would recover. But, as often happened in an age before people realised the importance of cleanliness, the wound festered. Nearly four weeks later, Sir Philip Sidney died.

## STATE FUNERAL FOR A COMMONER

When Sir Philip Sidney's body was brought back to England he was given a state funeral at St Paul's Cathedral. He was the first commoner ever to be given such a tribute. His coffin was carried by fourteen men and followed by a warhorse ridden by a boy carrying a broken lance.

Very few commoners have since been awarded such a privilege. These include: Lord Nelson, in 1805; the Duke of Wellington, in 1852; Lord Palmerston, in 1865; William Gladstone, in 1898; and – last but by no means least – Sir Winston Churchill in 1965. Before he died, Benjamin Disraeli was offered a state funeral but, in his will, he declined the honour.

# SHREWSBURY'S MOST SEVERE PLAGUE

**L**IKE THE REST of the country, Shropshire had been visited by the Black Death in the fourteenth century. From then on visitations of plague were a regular feature of life. We know, for example, of outbreaks in Shrewsbury in the 1500s and 1600s. The worst of these occurred in 1604, when one in every ten of the town's population died.

Of course, no one then understood the causes of these outbreaks – that it

*The house in the village of Grinshill built to accommodate Shrewsbury School in times of plague.*

was spread by rats' fleas. Consequently, whenever there was an outbreak of plague, orders were often circulated insisting that all stray animals – cats, dogs, even pigs – should be killed. This actually made things worse, as these animals would have killed the rats that carried the disease. Other orders were issued: as soon as there was a confirmed case in a household, the entire house would be closed up for a period of forty days, with guards to ensure that nobody tried to escape.

At the slightest sign of plague, shops and taverns would close. Anyone who had properties outside of town would instantly vacate his townhouse. In 1617, Shrewsbury School had a house built in the neighbouring village of Grinshill especially for use as a retreat for the pupils and staff should plague arrive in the town.

It wasn't until the nineteenth century that the real cause of plague was recognised. By this time, people had started to realise the importance of good hygiene in general. People were finally beginning to wash their hands before working with food or eating a

## BODIES IN THE BOATHOUSE

Not all people who suffered from the plague were left to die, perhaps alone and unattended, in their homes. Some were taken to isolation units around the outskirts of the town. One such isolation unit was the Boathouse Inn, which was used for victims from within the parish of St Chad's. Once you'd caught the plague, however, chances were that you would die. When people were dying in large numbers there was usually little care taken over how their bodies were disposed of: large pits were often dug and the bodies thrown unceremoniously into them. One such pit is said to have been dug in the churchyard of St Mary's church.

*The Boathouse Inn in the 1930s.*

meal. Clean drinking water was at last becoming available. Incredibly, water was pumped into the town from the English Bridge until the mid-1800s – in other words, Shrewsbury had been pumping its drinking water from a point where it would already have passed through the town's effluent, which was further upstream. By then, too, water sewers were being built under the ground instead of following natural contours in the ground down the middle of the street – Gullet Passage (which ran from the Square in the centre of Shrewsbury to Mardol and thence into the river) was well named.

# AD 1628

# THE IGNOMINIOUS DEATH OF A FORMER SHREWSBURY SCHOOLBOY

IN 1561 TWO seven-year-old boys arrived for their first day at Shrewsbury School: one a boy called Philip, and the other a boy called Fulke. The two lost and nervous boys instantly formed a friendship that was to last all of their lives.

Fulke Greville was born in 1554 near Alcester. The son of Sir Fulke Greville, a well-to-do country gentleman, he was related to the Earls of Westmorland. Greville grew up to become one of the most amazing men of his time.

*Riggs Hall, the only remaining part of the original wooden school foundation.*

From Shrewsbury School Fulke Greville went on to Cambridge University and then into the service of Queen Elizabeth I. He soon became a great favourite of hers. He served as a soldier and as a sailor and travelled (probably as a spy) all over Europe. In 1599, he was made a rear-admiral and put in charge of the largest vessel in the English fleet.

A few years later, with the arrival of King James I, his fortunes changed. James came to England with a retinue of his own and quickly made a clean sweep of as many of Elizabeth's men as he could. However, things improved for Greville in 1614, when he became Chancellor of the Exchequer; in 1621, he became the 1st Baron Brooke. By this time he had acquired Warwick Castle, subsequently paying the then enormous sum of £20,000 in order to renovate it and make it suitable to live in. As he died without heirs, the castle passed to his nephew and subsequent generations.

As for his death: one morning, as Greville was getting dressed in Holborn, London, his manservant attacked him, stabbing him twice in his side before turning the knife on himself. No one

Above  *Shrewsbury School today, now Shrewsbury Library.*

Below  *These statues show schoolboys in the original uniforms of the 1500s and 1600s.*

# WAS FULKE GREVILLE THE TRUE AUTHOR OF SHAKESPEARE'S PLAYS?

There are many people who insist that William Shakespeare, the son of a Stratford leatherworker, could not possibly have had the scholarship, knowledge of the world and sheer linguistic skills to have written the works attributed to him.

Several other writers have been put forward and, of all of them, Fulke Greville is one of the best qualified to take the honour. He actually lived in the same street as Shakespeare, and shared the same circle of friends (including people like Christopher Marlowe and Francis Bacon). Both grew up within only a few miles of each other, so Greville would have shared Shakespeare's intimate knowledge of places such as the Forest of Arden. Furthermore, in his own papers Greville gave clear hints that he had written the play *Antony and Cleopatra*. Could he have written them all?

The tomb of Fulke Greville. (With kind permission of the Thomas Fisher Rare Book Library, University of Toronto)

Fulke Greville was an accomplished poet, and wrote a life of his friend Sir Philip Sidney. These are a far cry from the style of the Shakespeare plays. However, had Greville written the plays it is perfectly feasible that he would not have wanted to own to them – writing plays was considered a very lowly occupation at the time, very much below that of a man of Greville's standing.

On the other hand, Shakespeare's father rose to become one of Stratford's aldermen. This was a position that meant he could take advantage of free education for his son at the local grammar school. Here, a young William would have received very much the same kind of education as Greville did at Shrewsbury. It is true that he did not then go on to university (Greville went to Cambridge); instead, in William Shakespeare's life there is a gap of several years when we know nothing about where he was or what he was doing – presumably he was studying at what is often known as 'the University of Life', and many men have become great that way.

As for the rest – well, considering Greville's full career as a judge, admiral in the navy, army captain, spy, courtier at Queen Elizabeth's court and Chancellor of the Exchequer for a time under James I, when did he get the time?

knows for certain why the servant, Ralph Haywood, stabbed him. One suggestion is that Greville, who was then seventy-four years of age, had been preparing his will and revealed that no provision had been made for Haywood, despite his many years of service.

Fulke Greville did not die immediately. He was taken back to Warwick Castle and, like his old school friend Philip Sidney, lingered in agony for a month. He eventually died in the Watergate Tower of the castle which, ever since, is reputed to be haunted by him. Greville's body was laid to rest in St Mary's church in Warwick. His tomb, in the Beauchamp Chapel, has written on it the words FULKE GREVILL, SERVANT TO QUEENE ELIZABETH, COUNCELLOR TO KING JAMES AND FRIEND TO SIR PHILIP SIDNEY. For all that Sidney had died over forty years before, the friendship that had started when both boys were only seven years old was still important.

# AD 1645

# THE CIVIL WAR COMES TO SHREWSBURY

**W**HEN THE CIVIL War broke out in 1642, Shrewsbury – and indeed most of Shropshire – supported the Royalist cause. It wasn't long after he had raised his standard in Nottingham that King Charles I arrived in the town.

He was welcomed with open arms, and anyone in the town who supported the Parliamentarian cause (and there must have been many) quietly looked the other way. Charles stayed in the Council House while he was here, and many of his entourage were billeted in Shrewsbury School, just across the road, or with local people.

King Charles was looking to the townspeople for money for his cause and his coffers were quickly filled with silver, which was then melted and minted into new coins and used to pay his soldiers. The King then departed, leaving a military presence in the town (which, for a time, was under the orders of his nephew, Prince Rupert).

But the town was never totally peaceful. Many people, even those who supported the Royalist cause, resented having the soldiers billeted with them – for one thing, it meant that they were forced to cover any expenses this entailed (including board and lodging for the soldiers, and for their horses too). On one occasion there was an explosion when a store of gunpowder blew up – many assumed that this was the result of a deliberate attack.

*Charles I, who stayed at the Council House. (With kind permission of the Thomas Fisher Rare Book Library, University of Toronto)*

*The Prince Rupert Hotel, where the man himself had his headquarters whilst staying in the town.*

Then, in February 1645, the town was attacked. The attack was totally unexpected yet was carried out suspiciously easily, leading to the obvious assumption that a traitor within the town had assisted the attackers.

It was in the middle of a long, cold winter's night when a group of eight carpenters were ferried along a stretch of the River Severn and landed just under the castle, close to St Mary's Water Lane. Once they had landed they proceeded to saw down a wooden palisade. This is not something that can be done silently. In fact, it would have been impossible for whoever was on duty in the nearby gatehouse not to have heard the sound of the saws – unless, that is, he deliberately ignored them.

The palisade was breached, and through it went two bodies of soldiers. The first was led by a local man called John Benbow, who had joined the Parliamentary army. Benbow was the son of a local tanner who lived in Mardol. He had enlisted in the Parliamentary army soon after the outbreak of the Civil War, and it was inevitable that, with his local knowledge, he should have been one of the men to lead the attack on Shrewsbury. His group scaled up the steep slope and entered the castle. The second group of men walked up St Mary's Water Lane and opened the north gate of the town (where a third group of soldiers was waiting) before going on to take control of the town itself. By morning the town and castle were in Parliamentarian hands. The whole thing had been relatively bloodless

## THE LOAN FROM SHREWSBURY SCHOOL

Tradition has it that while he was in the town King Charles persuaded the governors of Shrewsbury School to lend him £60. The usual promissory note was signed but the debt was never paid.

Over 200 years later, Shrewsbury School was moving to new premises on the outskirts of town and it was realised that if this loan (plus, of course, any interest) was repaid it would be extremely helpful. An application was therefore made to the Government for repayment. I leave it to you to guess the Government's response...

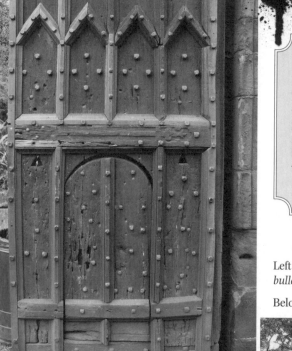

The phrase 'turncoat', a name for a traitor, dates back to the sixteenth century. It came about because a man, pretending he was no longer with a particular group of soldiers, would turn his coat inside out in order to hide his true colours.

Left  *Signs of the times: a gate with Civil War bullet holes in it.*

Below  *Traitor's Gate: St Mary's Water Lane.*

and from then on Shrewsbury remained in Parliamentarian hands until the end of the war.

But it wasn't entirely bloodless. Amongst the soldiers who were garrisoning the castle were thirteen Irish soldiers, who were hanged. Their crime was simply that they were Irish Catholics, enough for them to be hated by the Puritan regime. Prince Rupert retaliated, hanging thirteen of his prisoners in Whitchurch the following month.

As for St Mary's Water Lane – it may have that name on the street sign but, ever since then, it's been known to locals as Traitor's Gate.

Benbow served with the Parliamentary army for a number of years. Then, in 1649, he changed sides. He wasn't the only man to do so at the time: the execution of King Charles I in January made many Parliamentarians change their allegiance. Executing a King, anointed in the sight of God, was thought by many to be taking things too far.

This meant that at the Battle of Worcester (in 1651), Benbow was fighting for the Royalist cause. This battle was a total disaster for the Royalists and, inevitably, Benbow was captured. Considered a turncoat by his captors, he was taken to Chester, where he was tried for treason. He was found guilty and

*Captain Benbow's grave.*

taken back to his home town, where he was executed by firing squad just below the castle, in the very spot where he had scrambled up the walls some six years before.

Remarkably enough, his family was afterwards given his body and allowed to bury it with decency. He lies in the churchyard of Old St Chad's.

# AD 1685

# BLOODY ASSIZES

**A** FORMER SCHOOLBOY OF Shrewsbury School oversaw one of the bloodiest eras in British history.

George Jeffreys was born in 1648 in Wrexham and was aged about seven when he was first sent to Shrewsbury School. He stayed for no more than four years before going on to St Paul's School in London and then to Cambridge University. He never graduated at Cambridge but, instead, returned to London to study law.

Once he had been called to the Bar in 1668 he rose rapidly, becoming known as 'a master of cross-examination'. He acquired powerful patrons and soon was wealthy enough to buy several estates, playing host on one occasion to King Charles II himself. Still aged only thirty when he was appointed as Recorder of London, he was thirty-three when he became Lord Chief Justice of England and was a Privy Counsellor a couple of years later.

In an age when religious principles ruled everything, he seemed, at first, to be fairly moderate. Although a Protestant himself, he was always very much aware that Roman Catholicism did not automatically equate with treason. Many people throughout the 1600s would have strongly disagreed with Jeffreys on this point.

These religious differences came to a head throughout England in 1685 when King Charles II died and was succeeded by his openly Roman Catholic brother, James II. A Catholic on the throne of England was too much for many to accept and, within months, the Duke of Monmouth, an illegitimate son of Charles II, landed at Lyme Regis and proclaimed himself King. He began to march towards London but was met and defeated by the King's forces at the Battle of Sedgemoor. Monmouth was captured and taken to London, where he was executed within days. (It was said, incidentally, to have taken several blows with the axe to sever his head from his body.)

The leader may have been destroyed but his followers were still at large, still being rounded up and still needing to be punished. It was then that Judge George Jeffreys was appointed as the leader of four judges who were to visit the West

Country and oversee the trials of anyone who was suspected of supporting the Duke of Monmouth. It wasn't long before Jeffreys acquired the nickname that he is best remembered by – the Hanging Judge.

One of the first trials he held was that of Dame Alice Lisle in Winchester. An elderly lady who had never been anywhere near the battlefield, Alice was accused by association, having taken a few rebels who were on the run into her house and hidden them. She was found guilty and sentenced to be burnt at the stake. Jeffreys seems to have had second thoughts about this verdict, however, and deliberately delayed Dame Alice's execution whilst he sought the King's pardon for her. King James refused, and Dame Alice was executed, although her sentence was commuted to beheading. Jeffreys was vilified for his part in the tragedy. (Indeed, in 1689, when William III and Mary succeeded to the throne, one of the first actions of the new Parliament was to reverse the judgement. A bit late for Dame Alice, however...)

Meanwhile, Jeffreys proceeded westwards, holding trials in Dorchester, Taunton and Wells. Around 2,600 prisoners had been taken. Nearly half of them confessed that they had been involved in the rebellion, and so never came before the court: their punishments were meted out immediately. However, some 1,400 people ended up in the dock and, on being found guilty, were sentenced to death. On one day alone in Dorchester he condemned nearly 100 people to death. It's no wonder this series of trials has come to be known as 'the Bloody Assizes'.

As he arrived in the individual towns where the cases were to be heard, Jeffreys would instruct the local Council to prepare for the executions. The Councils were:

...to erect a gallows in the most public place; to (then) provide a sufficient number of faggots to burn the bowels of the said Traitors; to provide a furnace or cauldron to boil their heads and quarters, tar to tar them with, and spears and poles to fix and place their heads and quarters [for displaying].

*Judge Jeffreys discovered in London.*

Between 200 and 300 men were executed in England. The rest had their sentences commuted and were consigned to what can only be described as a living death – they were transported to work as slaves, most of them in the sugar-cane fields of the West Indies. Few survived, and those that did would have envied those who had died earlier of typhus whilst still in prison.

Some give, as an excuse for Jeffreys' strictness, the fact that he was in considerable pain from ill health at the time of the trials and was therefore less inclined to be lenient – he was suffering from kidney and bladder stones. Whether or not this is a valid point I leave you to judge for yourself.

Four years after Monmouth's rebellion there was another, more successful, revolt, led this time by Charles II's son-in-law, William of Orange. Known as the Glorious Revolution, this finally forced James II off the throne. With his main protector gone, George Jeffreys was totally exposed. He tried to escape from London by disguising himself as a sailor and heading for the docks to get a ship to take him to France. He was betrayed. Fortunately for him, he was then arrested by soldiers – ordinary people would probably have lynched him on the spot.

Jeffreys was locked up in the Tower of London to await trial on a charge of treason – the same charge that he had used against all those rebels after Sedgemoor. He died whilst in prison as a result of the kidney and bladder diseases that had troubled him for so long. When they heard of his death, the London mob made an effigy of his body, put it up on a gibbet and then burnt it.

A year later, in 1690, there was a general Act of Parliament giving a pardon to all former supporters of James – Judge Jeffreys' name, however, was deliberately omitted.

## JUDGE SIR GEORGE JEFFREYS, BARON OF WEM

Judge Jeffreys' association with Shropshire is not solely due to the few years during which he attended Shrewsbury School.

In 1684, King James II had awarded him with a baronetcy and it was around this time that Jeffreys learnt that the manor of Wem and Loppington in northern Shropshire was on the market. He bought the manor for £9,000 and so became the 1st Baron of Wem. He never actually visited the place, however.

*Judge Sir George Jeffreys, Baron of Wem.*

## PRISON FEVER

Prisons have never been intended to be places of comfort but in the past they were places of extreme horror – and not always intentionally so. Punishments in such places were bad enough, but many inmates were also regularly struck by what came to be known as gaol fever. This was probably typhus, spread by lice, but at the time no one knew its cause and it was often believed to be the result of witchcraft or poisons.

The filth of such places meant that once it took hold whole prison populations would quickly suffer – and not just the prisoners and warders. In one case in Oxford in 1577 it caused the deaths (within forty hours) of a number of judges, jurors and witnesses; it then spread into the town as well.

# SPIRITS OF SHREWSBURY

## The Dun Cow Murder and the Man who was Buried Alive!

**I**N 1688, THE 'Glorious Revolution' took place and the Roman Catholic King James II was finally ousted from the throne. In his place the Government invited James's daughter, Mary, and her husband, William, the Dutch Prince of Orange, to become joint monarchs.

The couple arrived in England early the following year, accompanied by numerous Dutch hangers-on, some of whom eventually found their way to Shrewsbury. One Dutch soldier in the service of King William found himself staying at the Dun Cow Inn in Abbey Foregate. There had for years been an

*The Dun Cow.*

# THE HISTORY OF EXECUTIONS IN SHREWSBURY

In early years, executions at Shrewsbury Prison were carried out in public: for a time, this was done on the top of the gatehouse at the entrance to Shrewsbury Prison.

The prison was built in 1793 and in the years that followed people would come to watch the executions from the open land between the prison and Shrewsbury Castle where, as one chronicler in 1841 described it, the people would congregate 'as they would to a bull-baiting or a cockfight'. This was a large area with a number of buildings around it, giving an excellent view of anything that was happening on the gatehouse. One of those buildings was a school – the Lancastrian Boys School – and it does not take much imagination to guess with what glee the boys at the school would have anticipated such an event. Their headmaster, however, was of another mind. He was so disturbed by the prospect of the boys in his care being emotionally upset by what they saw that he wrote to the prison's governor to request that executions be held only on days that the school was closed. I, however, have a distinct impression that the boys, knowing an execution was due to take place, would have been literally fighting each other for the best window seats in their classrooms.

It was not just the boys who enjoyed the show. In 1848, the school was replaced with the new Shrewsbury railway station, built on the same site. From then on, the executions could be seen from the station platforms. In those days, of course, it was not only the people travelling on the trains who required a ticket: those people who wanted to see them off would also have required a platform ticket. The usual cost of this was a penny, but on execution days the cost rose to tuppence.

One young boy who went along to watch the show, however, did not enjoy it. His name was Gathorne Hardy and he grew up to become the 1st Earl of Cranbrook and to serve in the Government as Home Secretary. In 1868, he introduced a Bill to make such practices private.

*Shrewsbury Prison.*

## OTHER EXECUTIONS AT SHREWSBURY PRISON

Altogether, seven people were executed by hanging in Shrewsbury Prison in the twentieth century. In every case, bar one, the murder victim was a woman; the exception was the lover of another victim.

There were four executions in the 1950s, all carried out by perhaps the most famous of British executioners, Albert Pierrepoint. In a career lasting less than twenty-five years, Pierrepoint executed 435 men and women; they included 202 Nazi war criminals condemned as a result of the war trials that followed the end of the Second World War.

The last person executed in Shrewsbury was George Riley, a twenty-one-year-old butcher's apprentice who lived opposite his victim, Adeline Mary Smith, a sixty-two-year-old widow. He had broken into her house in search of money, a fact that saw him hanged. His crime took place in 1960. In 1957, capital punishment had been abolished for many crimes in England. However, one capital offence remained: a murder that was carried out as part of a robbery. Despite the fact that George Riley fled the crime scene empty-handed, he was still found guilty of the double crime of robbery and murder because he confessed that robbery had been his aim. As he signed his confession, George is alleged to have said, 'I'm signing my own death warrant, aren't I?' And he was.

inn on this site. Indeed, the first one was probably built centuries before to provide accommodation for pilgrims.

No one knows exactly what happened, but it appears that the Dutchman quarrelled with a steward of Sir Richard Prynce, a powerful local man who owned numerous properties in the area. A fight broke out and Sir Richard's steward was killed.

On the orders of Sir Richard, the Dutchman was immediately court-martialled, found guilty and ordered to be hanged. He was led out to a hastily erected scaffold in the yard of the Dun Cow and complained vociferously all the way. He was a Dutch soldier in the service of the King; the steward was merely a servant. What did a servant's life matter in comparison with his own? Why should he be executed to atone for the murder of one Englishman of no importance?

But executed he was.

That Dutch soldier has never left the Dun Cow. He is seen regularly haunting the main rooms on the ground floor. He's not alone, however. There's a second ghost, a monk, who haunts the pub (although he tends to be seen downstairs, in the cellars, where he once would have looked after the kegs of ale... ).

The Lion Hotel, sitting halfway up Wyle Cop, was always Shrewsbury's most important coaching inn. From here regular services ran to towns and cities all over the country. The stabling at the back of The Lion, now the hotel's car park, had space for numerous horses.

On one occasion a man arrived on the stagecoach and took a night's accommodation. The following morning the chambermaid discovered him lying dead in his bed. She immediately raised the alarm. A search was then made through the dead man's belongings, but nothing was found to indicate who he was, where he had come from or where he was heading. However, there was enough money in his purse to pay for a decent burial so the innkeeper decided to call the undertaker to prepare the man for his burial. The innkeeper, quite naturally, wanted to keep all his other guests in ignorance of this sad event and arrangements were made that the burial service would be held as quickly, and quietly, as possible.

Right  *The Lion Hotel.*

Below  *St Julian's churchyard, where a man was buried alive.*

## BELLS IN THE CHURCHYARD

A deep coma can confuse many a medical practitioner to this day, so that it's no surprise that it was a common fear in the past that people might be buried alive. Consequently it became a regular practice, when someone was laid in his coffin, for a string to be tied around the wrist; this string would then run through a hole in the top of the coffin and up through the earth and be attached to a bell above the grave in the churchyard. Then, if the corpse revived, just a simple shaking of the wrist would cause the bell to ring and alert any passers-by.

No wonder churchyards are now considered to be places to fear. Walking past a churchyard on a gusty night, with bells ringing left, right and centre, must have been an unnerving experience.

That same day, the stranger was buried in St Julian's churchyard, just up the street from the hotel.

For the following two nights, moans and groans emanated from the churchyard – and they seemed to be coming from the vicinity of the newly buried coffin. Eventually a decision was made to unearth the coffin and find out just what was causing the noise. A frightful sight was revealed when the coffin was opened: all over the underside of the coffin lid there were grooves where the stranger had tried to scratch his way out of his wooden prison – to no avail. He had died, in the end, of asphyxiation. There was nothing more that could be done for him, and so his coffin was laid back in the ground and reinterred.

This poor stranger haunts the churchyard to this day.

# DEATH OF ADMIRAL BENBOW

JOHN BENBOW WAS born in Shrewsbury in around 1653, soon after his uncle had been executed for treason. He was already twenty-five when he joined the Royal Navy, and within a few years was commanding the HMS *Nonsuch*, sailing in waters around Africa and in the Mediterranean. In 1681, he and the captain of another ship attacked and captured an Algerian warship. Arguments then arose as to which of the English crews should have the prize money. When he lost the argument, Benbow quit the Royal Navy and joined the Merchant Navy instead.

He was soon once again in Mediterranean waters and in 1687 his

*Admiral Benbow, as portrayed on a Shropshire pub sign.*

The opening chapter of Robert Louis Stevenson's *Treasure Island* takes place in an inn run by Jack Hawkins and his mother. The inn is named *The Admiral Benbow*. In fact, there are numerous pubs up and down the country that bear his name.

ship, the *Malaga Merchant*, was attacked by Moorish pirates. Benbow beat off the attack and afterwards cut off the heads of thirteen pirates who had been killed on board his ship, salting them to preserve them. With this evidence of his victory he sailed for Cadiz to claim a reward from the magistrates there.

Word of Benbow's exploits spread and he was once again offered a commission in the Royal Navy. He rejoined and rose steadily through the ranks. By 1701, in which year Benbow became a vice-admiral, he was in the West Indies with seven ships under his command, searching for a French squadron of four warships and three transports under Admiral Jean du Casse, who was raiding English and Dutch shipping. Finally, in August 1702, the French fleet was sighted but light winds meant that the English fleet had been scattered and it took them some time to regroup in order to engage with the enemy.

Battle was eventually joined. However, after only two hours nightfall caused the fleets to break off. The following day Benbow wanted to recommence the attack but the captains of five of the ships under his command refused to close, leaving only two ships, the *Breda* and the *Ruby*, tracking the French fleet (although a third captain, on board the *Falmouth*, also joined them). The chase lasted for four days, by which time the *Ruby* had been disabled. Benbow ordered it to retire. A shanty of the time records Benbow's heroics:

> Brave Benbow he set sail for to fight, for
> to fight.
> Brave Benbow he set sail for to fight.
> Brave Benbow he set sail with a fine
> and pleasant gale
> But his captains they turned tail in a
> fright, in a fright.

Finally, the entire French fleet attacked the *Breda* and it was then that Benbow was hit by chain-shot, breaking his leg. He insisted that a hammock should be tied up on the deck so that he could continue to mastermind the attack on the French.

> Brave Benbow lost his legs by chain
> shot, by chain shot,
> Brave Benbow lost his legs by chain
> shot.
> Brave Benbow lost his legs, and all on
> his stumps he begs,
> 'Fight on my English lads, 'Tis our lot,
> 'tis our lot.'

> The surgeon dressed his wounds, cries
> Benbow, cries Benbow,
> The surgeon dressed his wounds, cries
> Benbow,
> 'Let a cradle now in haste, on the
> quarterdeck be placed,
> That the enemy I may face 'til I die, 'til
> I die.'

*Local tradition has it that when John Benbow left Shrewsbury he left his door key attached to a nail in a nearby tree. He was away for such a long time that the key had become embedded in the tree by the time he returned, as can be seen.*

Eventually, however, the English captains regrouped and insisted that Benbow abandon the fight because 'after six days of battle ... the men were exhausted, there was a general lack of ammunition, the ships' rigging and masts were badly damaged, and the winds were generally variable and undependable.'

Benbow was forced by his captains to concede.

The English fleet returned to Jamaica and, on arrival there, Benbow had his captains imprisoned to await a court-martial for cowardice. Even the French admiral, du Casse, had anticipated that the English fleet would be successful. He wrote a letter to Benbow in which he said that he 'had little hopes on Monday last but to have supped in your cabin: but it pleased God to order otherwise. I am thankful for it. As for those cowardly captains who deserted you, hang them up, for by God they deserve it.'

The captains were all found guilty at the court-martial but their sentences were deferred until they returned to England. There, they were confirmed by the Crown, one captain being

*Memorial to the Admiral in St Mary's church.*

imprisoned before eventually being pardoned and the other two being shot.

Admiral Benbow, meanwhile, remained in Jamaica. He never recovered from the wound he had received to his leg, and suffered from a severe depression as a result. He died in Jamaica and lies buried in Kingston.

# AD 1739

# ICARUS OF THE ROPE DIVES TO HIS DEATH!

**I**N JANUARY 1739, handbills were circulated around Shrewsbury advertising an exciting spectacle that would take place at St Mary's church on 2 February:

> This is to give notice to all lovers of art and ingenuity, that the famous Robert Cadman intends to fly off St Mary's spire over the Severn on Saturday next, firing two pistols, and acting several tricks upon the rope which will be very diverting to the spectators.
>
> The abovesaid Robert Cadman having no one but his wife to collect what money Gentlemen and Ladies are pleased to give him, desires the favour of those who are at a distance, either to send their servants with it, or he intends to wait on them at their own homes.

Robert Cadman was a steeplejack and ropewalker who, when working on steeples and high towers, would augment his income by performing tricks on the ropes that he used while he was working. He had acquired the title of 'Icarus of the Rope' after he had slid, face-down, from the cupola of St Paul's Cathedral in London while blowing a trumpet.

His exploits hadn't been without accidents. One time he was halfway down the rope at a church near Devizes in Wiltshire when the spire to which it was attached gave way. On that occasion his fall had been broken when he landed in a tree, and he escaped with only minor injuries. One would think that such an accident would make him take more care – but perhaps, having survived one such accident, he might have thought he was indestructible?

Cadman was invited to Shrewsbury to take down the cock on the top of the spire and replace it. Performing from Shrewsbury's spire, which was one of the tallest in the country, was an opportunity Cadman could not miss. His plan was to attach a rope some 800ft long (250m) from the ground in the Gaye Meadow across the River Severn, and tie it through a louver in the spire. Having tied the rope firmly, Cadman's usual routine was to then walk up the rope from ground level, performing tricks as he went. Once he reached the top, the

Let this small Monument record the name
Of CADMAN. and to future times proclaim
How by'n attempt to fly from this high spire
Across the Sabrine stream he did acquire
His fatal end. 'Twas not for want of skill
Or courage to perform the task he fell:
No, no, a faulty Cord being drawn too tight
Hurried his Soul on high to take her flight
Which bid the Body here beneath good Night.
Feb.ʳʸ 2.ⁿᵈ 1739 aged 28.

*A poetically written memorial now sits besides the west door of St Mary's church. However, a Shrewsbury schoolboy was probably most accurate when he chalked underneath the memorial, 'Goodnight, goodnight, poor Bob Cadman; you lived and died just like a madman.'*

grand finale for his performance would be his descent. For this he would tie a wooden breastplate around his chest. Along the breastplate a groove had been cut, so that Cadman could lie down with the rope in the groove. He would then slide back down to the ground with his arms outstretched, firing his pistols as he went.

But he had no sooner started to slide down the rope from St Mary's spire than the rope broke. He plummeted to the ground. It transpired that the break had been caused because the rope that had been tied to the steeple had been badly frayed by rubbing against the stonework.

An account in the *Gloucester Journal* reported that Cadman had been warned about the possibility of this happening but had ignored the advice, saying that 'although he was a very daring fellow in his way [he] was grown too daring, for notwithstanding he was frequently cautioned by people here, he would not be prevailed upon to so much as set anything between the rope and the stone to prevent it cutting off.'

Incidentally, notice how, in that handbill, Cadman states that his wife will be there to collect money from the audience. That lady was no fool. When Cadman fell she ensured that she collected as much money as she could before the crowd could disperse. Having done that, she then went to check on her husband – only to find that she had just collected her widow's pension.

## ST MARY'S SPIRE

St Mary's church was founded in Saxon times but the present church is a wonderful conglomeration of different styles of architecture through the centuries, beginning with the time when the Normans started to rebuild in the twelfth century.

At the western end of the church there sits a 78ft-high Norman tower and it was on top of this, in the 1470s, that a spire was eventually built. This spire was 145ft tall, making it, when it was completed, the third tallest spire in

*St Mary's spire.*

England. No wonder Robert Cadman saw it as such a challenge.

Looking at the spire today it is evident, from the lighter colour of the stone, that the top section of it has at some time been repaired.

The night of 11 February 1894 saw tremendous gales covering much of the country. In Shrewsbury the wind was already such that, by midday, the *Shrewsbury Chronicle* recorded that, 'its fury [created] general terror and alarm. It was almost impossible to walk along the streets so exceedingly rough was the wind; it was very dangerous too, for bricks, tiles and slates were being dashed from the housetops in all directions.'

That evening the storm got worse, and at 9.30 p.m. there was a sudden crash 'resembling the discharge of a cannon' and the top 40ft of the spire fell through the roof of the nave to the ground.

It so happened that this disaster to St Mary's church happened at just the same time that the people of the town were raising money to erect a statue in honour of the town's most famous son, Charles Darwin. Many people to this day disagree with Darwin's theories of evolution and this was even more the case in the 1890s. The vicar of St Mary's, the Revd Newdigate Poyntz, was one such, and the Sunday following the crash he preached a sermon saying that the damage showed the anger of the Almighty and was a judgement on the townsfolk for daring to subscribe.

The following week the *Shrewsbury Chronicle*, however, disagreed, reporting that the 'fall would have been much more impressive... had it happened on a windless night. Furthermore, had it happened at St Chad's, where the vicar is supporting the memorial, it would seem more appropriate.' The statue was eventually unveiled in 1897 and sits outside the town's library, once the school that Darwin attended as a boy.

# AD 1749

# JACOBITE SPY EXECUTED IN SHREWSBURY

THOMAS ANDERSON WAS a supporter of the Stuart cause in the years of the Jacobite rebellions that followed the accession of the German George I to the throne of England and Scotland.

Born in 1720 near Richmond in Yorkshire, he was well educated and travelled widely. Indeed, it may have been on his travels to the Continent that he became involved with the Jacobite cause. England at this time was awash with rumours of rebellions against the newly installed Hanoverian king.

In 1746, Thomas Anderson enlisted in Sir John Ligonier's Regiment of

*St Mary's church today – Anderson's grave is in the foreground.*

# DID THE SECRET SERVICE ARRANGE A MURDER IN SHREWSBURY?

───❄───

It is generally agreed that Thomas Anderson was guilty. Occasionally, however, people who are entirely innocent become caught up in a web of intrigue, causing questions to which there seem to be no clear answers. On 24 March 1984 the body of a woman was found on Haughmond Hill, overlooking Shrewsbury. It was that of seventy-eight-year-old Hilda Murrell, who had disappeared from her home a few days beforehand.

As soon as her body was found, rumours started to circulate. Miss Murrell was a well-known and popular figure in the town, where she had lived all her life. Her grandfather had founded a garden nursery which Hilda had taken over in 1937 and, in the years that followed, she had become a world authority on roses, winning awards at flower shows all over England. In 1970 she retired, selling the business to a man who would soon become even better known in the world of horticulture – Percy Thrower.

But retirement for Hilda Murrell did not mean sitting in an armchair doing nothing. She had long been interested in everything to do with Shropshire's history and its countryside. She was a founding member of the Shropshire Wildlife Trust, had been involved in the founding of the National Soil Association and she frequently worked for the Council for the Protection of Rural England.

Along the way she became concerned, also, about the risks associated with the use of nuclear energy, paying particular attention to the problems of disposing of radio-active waste. In 1978 she wrote an article titled 'What Price Nuclear Power?' When, the following year, there was a disaster at the American nuclear plant at Three Mile Island, all her concerns were shown to be justified. From then on, she turned her attentions to the safety aspects of using nuclear power.

Meanwhile, a second nuclear plant was proposed at Sizewell in Suffolk. The initial plans for this plant were very similar to those at the failed Three Mile Island site and Hilda Murrell began a campaign to force the Government to reconsider their plans. She wrote numerous articles, including a paper called 'An Ordinary Citizen's View of Radioactive Waste Management' which she planned to present to a planning inquiry into the new nuclear power plant.

Then, a few days before the inquiry was to be held, she disappeared. A search at her house revealed that some cash had been stolen and her car had been taken. There were witnesses who recalled seeing the car being driven erratically through the town by an unknown man. The car was found abandoned in a country lane, but it was another three days before her body was found in woodland not far away. She had been beaten, stabbed several times and then left to die of hypothermia.

Everyone recalled that she had been due to present her paper rubbishing the Government's plans for Sizewell. Had she been silenced by the British Secret Service? Had she been murdered as a warning to anyone trying to force an anti-nuclear agenda?

The truth, when it was finally uncovered, was rather more prosaic, but it took twenty years to come to light. By 2003 forensic techniques had developed enormously, meaning that the diagnosing of DNA samples from crime scenes had become a regular part of any murder investigation. A cold-case review of the murder discovered semen stains on the clothing that Hilda Murrell had been wearing and this evidence led to the arrest of a thirty-five-year-old labourer, Andrew George.

George was only sixteen at the time of the attack but it transpired that he had set out, that day in 1984, to rob Hilda Murrell's house. She had surprised him in the act, and he had turned on her, assaulting her before stabbing her three times. He had then stolen her car and taken her body to Haughmond, where he had dumped it. George tried to blame his brother for the murder, but there was no evidence to support this and so he was found guilty of murder and jailed for life.

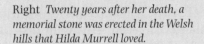

Right *Twenty years after her death, a memorial stone was erected in the Welsh hills that Hilda Murrell loved.*

Dragoons which had not long since been recalled to England because of Bonnie Prince Charlie's '45 Rebellion. The regiment, however, had not been involved in the Battle of Culloden, instead being based in the English Midlands. Soon after Anderson joined up, Ligonier was promoted to head the British section of an Allied army based in the Low Countries.

Three years later the regiment was back in England, in Worcester, and Anderson obtained several days' leave. He never returned. Instead he travelled to Europe, where he met other Jacobite sympathisers, and, from there, he went to Edinburgh as an agent for the cause, using the name Charles Douglas.

In Edinburgh he was arrested on suspicion of treason and interrogated by the Lord Provost. Nothing, however, could be proved against him and he was on the verge of being released when a letter addressed to him in his correct name was intercepted. It was then

*Thomas Anderson's grave.*

*Bonnie Prince Charlie, the 'Young Pretender'.*

discovered that he was wanted by the British Army for desertion and he was escorted to re-join his regiment.

Once back in Worcester he was court-martialled and sentenced to death. His regiment, meantime, had moved to Shrewsbury – and so it was in Shrewsbury that the sentence was carried out.

Accompanied by his former colleagues, he was marched in procession through the town to Kingsland, where he was executed by firing squad. Following the execution his body was taken to St Mary's church for burial. Feelings were high, however, not just amongst the townspeople but also amongst the soldiers of his regiment, who were disgusted by his support of the Jacobite cause. No one was prepared to take his body into the church for the burial service and eventually the vicar, the Revd Benjamin Wingfield, suggested that, 'if the army would not take the body to him at the church door, he would carry out the whole of the service at the graveside'.

Which was exactly what was done. The grave can still be seen in St Mary's churchyard. The Jacobite cause was dying by this time but, for many supporters, Thomas Anderson is seen as the last English Jacobite martyr.

# AD 1774

# CLIVE OF INDIA
## Shrewsbury MP Commits Suicide

**B**ORN IN 1725, Robert Clive was the son of a lawyer and the eldest of eight children. As a boy he was always in trouble. He was only seven years old when, one day, he decided to go up the tower of St Mary's church in Market Drayton; reaching the roof, he then clambered onto one of the gargoyles – from where he had an excellent view of everyone coming to attend a church service. He had with him a gazunder, full of the contents that – in the days before indoor plumbing – usually went into gazunders – and, with this, he pelted the churchgoers. (For those of you who don't know what a gazunder is, think in terms of a pot that *goes under* the bed – in other words, he had a chamber pot with him.)

Then, when still in his teens, Clive was in trouble once again – this time he and his gang of fellow Market Drayton hooligans decided to dam up a drain running along one of the town's streets, causing the filthy water to flood a butcher's shop. The butcher had apparently refused to pay the gang protection money.

What with his son also being expelled from three schools, it's no wonder that Clive's father was desperate to find him something to do well away from Shropshire. He found him a job as a clerk with the East India Company in Madras and so, at the age of eighteen, Clive set sail for India. The journey, dependent as it was on sea currents and winds, took several months. Clive was homesick, he was bored and – in a fit of depression – he attempted suicide, pointing a pistol at his head and pressing the trigger. Nothing happened, and so he decided that perhaps he was intended to live for rather longer.

Robert Clive arrived in India in the mid-1700s, at just the time when the British and the French were fighting each other for control of what was potentially a very rich possession, each side making pacts with various Indian Princes in order to pursue their interests. The East India Company's army offered far more excitement that sitting at a desk clerking and so Clive enlisted. He had at last found his ideal vocation.

Clive's courage under fire was soon noticed. He was mentioned in the despatches that were sent back to England. The Prime Minister,

Anti-clockwise, from left: *portrait of Robert Clive; Clive's statue in the Square, Shrewsbury; the statue today.*

William Pitt, once referred to him as 'a heaven-born general'. Clive was still only twenty-seven at the time.

In 1753 Clive, now married and well on the way to becoming extremely wealthy, returned to England. Boredom soon followed so that, when he was offered the post of Deputy Governor of Madras, Colonel Robert Clive immediately accepted. The war against the French continued and it was in June 1757 that the two armies faced each other for the last time. It seemed that everything was in favour of a French victory – their army consisted of 35,000 Indian infantry with 15,000 cavalry and fifty-three field guns. Clive's army, on the other hand, numbered less than 3,000 infantry (of whom there were 800 European troops) and eight guns. Yet clever tactics on Clive's part meant that it was he who was the victor at the Battle of Plassey. Clive was still only thirty-two years of age and now immeasurably wealthy thanks to the gifts of immense riches from those Indian Princes who supported the British.

Clive once again returned to England and entered politics, becoming MP for Shrewsbury and also the town's mayor.

His health by now was failing. It is thought that he suffered from manic depression and that his attempt at suicide may have been an early indication of this. Recalled once more to India in 1765, Clive was now also becoming dependent on opium to relieve his abdominal pains. His troubles didn't end with his health. The wealth that he had acquired led to a great deal of resentment and when, on his arrival in India, he started to investigate corruption, people started to question his own probity and the morality of just how he had acquired his own wealth. Back in England once again, Clive found himself facing corruption charges in court, charges of which he was finally cleared.

However, by this time he was suffering from severe depression, and even the fact that his good name had at last been restored was not enough to lift his mood. It was only a short time later that his wife discovered his blood-splattered body. Clive had finally succeeded in committing suicide. He had cut his throat. He was only forty-nine years of age.

The family did their best to hide the fact of his suicide – this was an age when to commit suicide was almost synonymous with committing murder, and the shame of such an act within one's family was just as great. Robert Clive's body was brought back to the village of Moreton Say, where he had

## ELECTION CORRUPTION IN THE 1700S

To become an MP in the 1700s was relatively easy – provided you had plenty of spare cash.

Today, when we have an election, everyone who has the vote attends a polling booth in his or her locality and voting is relatively simple. In the 1700s, however, if you wished to vote for a candidate in an election you had to travel from your home (perhaps some miles away) to the town where the election was being held. Why bother? So, in order to encourage you to attend and place your vote, the candidates who were standing for election would happily be prepared to pay for you to travel to the town, put you up in the local inn and provide you with food and drink while you were there. It was too good an opportunity for many people to miss. In fact, why not take the wife and kids along too and have a good time while you were there? With the free booze flowing, and everyone out to have a good time, it was no wonder that prisons were always full to overflowing at election time.

In one election that took place in Shrewsbury in 1796, two cousins, John Hill and William Noel-Hill, fought for the seat. Between them they spent somewhere in the region of £30,000: their accounts indicate that they spent £6,384 in the local pubs alone. The seat, incidentally, was won by William, who was the second son. He was subsequently told by his elder brother not to stand again – they would not be able to afford it. So William later entered the Diplomatic Service instead.

*Robert Clive's memorial in Moreton Say church.*

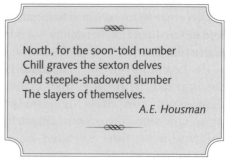

North, for the soon-told number
Chill graves the sexton delves
And steeple-shadowed slumber
The slayers of themselves.

*A.E. Housman*

been born, and buried somewhere in the church in the middle of the night with no marker upon his actual grave.

For years no one knew exactly where Clive was buried: the only reminder that he was somewhere nearby was a bronze plaque on the wall which stated simply that he was 'buried within the walls of this church'. However, during recent renovations in the church a sealed lead coffin was discovered. An application was made for permission to open the coffin and verify that it was indeed Robert Clive who was thus interred, but this was refused. But, with no indication on the coffin of who lay within, it seems probable that this is where Robert Clive now lies.

There has long been a degree of shame associated with suicide. In medieval times people who had committed suicide were (along with executed criminals) often buried in unmarked graves by crossroads. Because these were people who had been guilty of dastardly crimes, it was feared that they might come back to life and haunt those left behind. It was thought that if they were buried beside a crossroads, however, they would not know which road to follow to seek their revenge.

Furthermore, crossroad junctions were often the site of executions – the cross shape of the junction meant that it was as near to being consecrated ground as possible without being a churchyard. Perhaps the most famous execution site by a crossroads was that at Tyburn in London, a site that had been a crossroad junction since Roman times.

The quote above comes from the poem *Hughley Steeple* by A.E. Housman, in which Housman notes that the suicide's graves are on the northern side of the church. The north (or shadowed) side was traditionally reserved for unbaptised babies, unmarried girls who died in childbirth and criminals.

# AD 1788

# DISASTER AT ST CHAD'S CHURCH

**I**F **EVER YOU** study Norman churches and admire their towers and spires, you should never ask if the tower or spire has ever fallen down. Rather, you should ask *when* the tower or spire fell down. With shallow foundations and constant additions to earlier buildings that weren't built to carry over-heavy weights, such disasters were a constant occurrence.

St Chad's church in Shrewsbury was first founded some time in the late eighth century, but whatever Saxon church was there was knocked down and replaced by the Normans. The church the Normans built was enormous. It survived for several hundred years until, in the late 1700s, it began to show signs of age. Cracks were appearing in the structure, and occasionally bits of plaster would fall on the congregation during services. Eventually the Parish Council asked the recently appointed county surveyor of Shropshire to come along and carry out a survey.

This the young man did and, at a meeting afterwards, he condemned the structure totally, telling the Councillors that there was nothing they could do to save the building. Their only option was to pull it down and rebuild – an expensive option, particularly when local builders disagreed and said they could shore up the building and make it safe.

Not surprisingly, the local builders were then given a contract to do just that. However, only a week or so later, at around 4 a.m., there was a sudden, terrifying crash which woke most of the townspeople. Not only had the tower of the church fallen to the ground, but it had also brought the entire north side of the nave down with it.

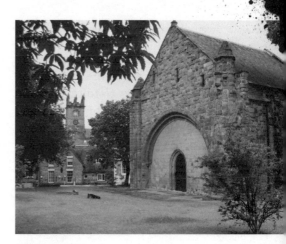

*Old St Chad's.*

## NEW ST CHAD'S AND THE USE OF IRON

All that remains of St Chad's today is the former Lady Chapel. It's now known as Old St Chad's since, following the collapse of the building, another St Chad's church has been built. New St Chad's, as it is called, was very advanced in both its design (it has a circular nave) and its construction. This was the period when the Industrial Revolution was at its height. Shropshire was where the first iron bridge was built, and the county in which the first iron rails were produced; it made the first iron wheels, the first iron boat and the first iron-framed multi-storey building. People were experimenting with the use of iron in many ways. St Chad's was built using iron columns.

*New St Chad's.*

It so happened that the previous evening the verger of the church had gone into the tower to toll the bell in advance of a funeral that was to be held the following day. While doing so, some of the stonework from the interior of the tower had fallen on him and he had run from the building in fear. If the crash had happened while he was tolling the bell for the funeral itself it would not have been just one man's death that the town mourned.

As for that young county surveyor whose advice everyone ignored? His name was Thomas Telford.

# THIRTY THINGS YOU DIDN'T KNOW ABOUT CHARLES DARWIN

- Charles Robert Darwin was born in Shropshire, not Staffordshire. Confusion often arises over his birthplace when people learn that both Darwin's parents and, later, his wife, all came from Staffordshire. But Charles was born in Shrewsbury.

- Darwin was born on the same day (12 February 1809) as Abraham Lincoln.

- Charles was named after his uncle, his father's eldest brother. Uncle Charles died as a result of contracting an infection when he was a medical student carrying out anatomical dissections. Despite his baptismal name, as a little boy Charles was known as Bobby within the family.

- One of Charles's early childhood memories was of watching a cavalry officer's funeral in the churchyard at New St Chad's. The officer's horse was present, with the officer's boots placed back-to-front in the stirrups. A salute was fired as the coffin was laid in the ground. A poignant memory for a young boy of eight, particularly since he had attended his mother's funeral only the month before.

- Darwin's grandfathers were both brilliant men and were members of that great eighteenth-century think tank known as the Lunar Society. Erasmus Darwin was one of the finest polymaths of the age and worked on subjects as diverse as the laws of gases and plant physiology; he invented a mechanical copying machine and was considered to be one of the finest poets of the age. Josiah Wedgwood is probably better known today because of the china company that he founded,

*Darwin's family home and birthplace.*

*Darwin's statue outside Shrewsbury library, once his school.*

but he also invented a pyrometer to measure kiln temperatures and experimented with new forms of chinaware.

☠ Both Darwin's grandfathers died before he was born. This was perhaps just as well – they certainly would not have been impressed by the young boy who showed no promise at all of any future abilities.

☠ Darwin's father, Dr Robert Darwin, was a very large and heavily built man. In fact, Charles once said that his father was 'the largest man he ever knew'. In fact, Robert Darwin always went down a flight of stairs backwards, as he feared toppling over otherwise. Occasionally, when visiting patients in their homes, he would send his coach driver into the house first to test the floors and stairs to check that they would stand his weight.

☠ As a schoolboy, Charles Darwin was given the nickname 'Gas'. This came about when the other boys learnt that Charles and his brother, Erasmus, had been carrying out chemistry experiments in a shed in the garden of their home, sometimes causing explosions (which must have delighted Erasmus and Charles, if not their father).

☠ Charles hated school. This is hardly surprising when you consider that the curriculum of the day consisted almost entirely of subjects like Greek, Latin and philosophy. Indeed, the headmaster at Shrewsbury School, Samuel Butler, didn't even consider mathematics to be very important. Darwin's interests, on the other hand, consisted entirely of natural history subjects – fossils, bugs, rocks...

☠ His father wanted Charles to become a doctor and so, at the age of sixteen, Charles went to Edinburgh University to study medicine. He did not enjoy it. He was appalled when he witnessed operations taking place – without anaesthetics in those days! After two years he left Edinburgh.

☠ When he was at Edinburgh, Charles learnt the skill of taxidermy from a freed slave from Guyana named John Edmonstone. This skill was to prove to be useful when later, on HMS *Beagle*, he wanted to preserve specimens to send back to England.

☠ Darwin gave his first scientific speech in 1827 while still a student at Edinburgh, at a meeting of the Plinian Society. It was about oyster shells and the larva of sea-mats.

- When he left Edinburgh, Darwin went on to Cambridge University to study theology, his father now intending that he should become a parson. When he took his final exams for his theology degree, Darwin came 10th out of 178 students.

- Charles Darwin's first love was a girl called Fanny Owen. She, however, had no wish to take second place to his interest in bugs and rocks and threw him over.

- When he received the invitation from Captin Fitzroy to join him on board the HMS *Beagle* as a naturalist, Charles at first refused. This was not his own choice, however: his father refused to give the then twenty-two-year-old Charles permission to go.

- It was only thanks to the intervention of his Uncle Jos (Josiah Wedgwood II) that Charles was able to persuade his father to allow him to go.

- When Darwin and Captain Fitzroy first met, Fitzroy had second thoughts about his invitation to Darwin to travel with him: he didn't like the shape of Darwin's nose, deciding that it signified that Darwin had an unstable character.

- Darwin's job as a naturalist on the HMS *Beagle* was not a paid one. He travelled as Fitzroy's companion, not as an employee of the Royal Navy, although it was a naval vessel that he travelled on.

- While in South America, Darwin allowed various flies and bugs to suck his own blood so that he could study how they did so. This, unfortunately, was probably what caused the ill health that dogged him for the rest of his life.

- For Darwin's twenty-fifth birthday, Captain Fitzroy named a mountain after him – Mount Darwin is the highest peak in the Tierra del Fuego.

- When his book, *On the Origin of Species*, was published on 24 November 1859, 1,250 copies of the book were printed. They sold out on the day of publication. The second edition consisted of 3,000 copies.

- The term 'Darwinism' for the process of evolution by natural selection was first coined by Thomas Huxley in 1860.

- Darwin was by no means the first person to think – or even write – on the subject of evolution. His grandfather, Erasmus Darwin, had previously published a paper on the same subject called 'Zoonomia'. What made Darwin's book so important was that he worked out a process by which evolution could occur, known as the survival of the fittest.

- Darwin published seventeen books of research altogether, his last one being a tome all about earthworms.

- Lord Palmerston proposed to Queen Victoria that Darwin should be given a knighthood. The idea was abandoned because Bishop Wilberforce (the Bishop of Oxford) disapproved.

- Charles's mother and wife were both talented pianists. This was all a bit wasted on Charles, who was tone deaf.

*Darwin in later life. (George Grantham Bain Collection, Library of Congress, LC-DIG-ggbain-03485)*

🕱 Darwin was a backgammon fiend and would play two games every night with his wife, Emma. He even kept a tally of the scores over the years that they played.

🕱 Charles and Emma had ten children. Darwin was particularly good with children. There is a delightful story of how, on one occasion, the children hacked several dead bugs apart and then glued bits of each of them together to make a new bug. This they presented to their father as a rare specimen they had just discovered in the garden. Darwin looked at the bug and asked the children, 'Did it hum when you found it?' 'Yes, Papa,' said one of the children. 'It certainly did.' 'In that case,' said Darwin, 'I think what you have found is a humbug.'

🕱 In 1874, Darwin attended a séance at his brother Erasmus's house. Also present was the author George Eliot, and Darwin's cousin, Francis Galton. The room got stuffy and Darwin went to lie down, thereby missing all the fuss.

🕱 When he died, Charles Darwin was buried in Westminster Abbey. This was very much against the wishes of his wife and family, who wanted him buried in the churchyard in the village of Downe, in Kent, where they lived.

# SECOND-IN-COMMAND AT THE BATTLE OF WATERLOO

**D**ADDY HILL WAS the Duke of Wellington's most trusted general.

Born in Prees in the north of Shropshire, Rowland Hill, to give him his correct name, was the second son of Sir John Hill, a member of an ancient Shropshire family, the Hills of Hawkstone Park. Educated at King's School in Chester, he enlisted in the army in 1790 at the age of eighteen. He served first in Ireland and then was posted to the Mediterranean where, in 1801, he was part of the force driving the French out of Egypt, during which campaign he was hit in the head with a musket ball. By 1805 he had reached the rank of Major-General.

It was in that same year that he first met Wellington and the two immediately became friends before, in 1808, Hill joined Wellington's forces in the Iberian Peninsula. It was there that Hill was to build his reputation. He was a brilliant tactician and would be much better known were it not for the fact that he was overshadowed by Wellington. But Wellington understood and came to rely on his skills, often giving Hill an independent command that he would not have entrusted to his other officers, even officers who were more senior.

In 1811, at the Battle of Arroyo des Molinos, Hill totally surprised the French general so that the French army was almost annihilated whilst Hill himself suffered relatively few casualties.

*A portrait of Lord Rowland Hill, better known as 'Daddy' Hill.*

*Marshall Soult, defeated by Hill in possibly his greatest victory.*

The following year he captured French fortifications at Almaraz and destroyed or took all the French armaments and supplies whilst, at the same time, destroying their line of communication.

It was in December 1813 that General Hill had his greatest victory during the Battle of the Nive in the Pyrenees. Hill found himself isolated on the east bank of the River Nive when a bridge collapsed. He was left with a force of 14,000 men and ten guns facing one of Napoleon Bonaparte's finest soldiers, Marshal Soult. Seeing Hill's precarious position, Soult immediately ordered six divisions (some 35,000 men) and twenty-two guns to attack. All night the Allied forces held off the French attack, with Hill encouraging his men at every point of danger, until – seeing, at last, the arrival of Wellington's reinforcements – the French fled. 'Hill, the day's your own,' Wellington said – and then, hearing that Hill (who never used profanities),

had actually been heard to swear during the battle, later said, 'If Hill has begun to swear, they must all mind what they are about.' In fact, it was said of Rowland Hill that he had only been heard to swear twice in his entire lifetime – the first time was when, during the Battle of Talavera, he had nearly been captured by a French soldier.

The Peninsular War finally ended in 1814 and Hill was then elevated to the peerage, becoming Baron of Almaraz and Hawkstone. He returned to Shropshire but with Napoleon's escape from Elba the following year, Hill was recalled and once again joined Wellington, this time in Brussels.

At the Battle of Waterloo, Hill was in charge of Wellington's right flank, from where he had to protect the only sure route to safety for the British army should Napoleon's troops succeed. Technically, he was the third most senior officer in the British army at the battle; Wellington was in overall charge and, leading the cavalry, was the Marquis of Anglesey. However, Wellington's orders were that, should he be killed in the battle, it was Hill who was delegated to take over command, not the Marquis. It never came to that, of course, and instead it was Hill who, for a time, was thought to have been killed. He led a charge against Napoleon's Imperial Guard towards the end of the battle in which his horse was shot beneath him. Fortunately, he escaped unwounded. (Incidentally, Hill had three brothers who were also on the field at Waterloo, all of whom survived.)

In the years that followed Waterloo, Hill was based in France for a time and then, in 1828, when the Duke of

Above *It is said that Lord Hill built the windmill pictured here as a replica of the one around which he had fought at Waterloo. It is now a private house.*

Right *Lord Hill's Column.*

Wellington became Prime Minister, he succeeded him as Commander-in-Chief of the British Army, holding this position until 1842 (when he resigned due to ill health). Lord Hill died that same year and is buried at Hadnall, just to the north of Shrewsbury.

## LORD HILL'S COLUMN

Standing just in front of Shrewsbury's Shire Hall, Lord Hill's Column is the tallest Doric column in England. Standing on a pedestal and flanked, like Nelson's (Corinthian style) Column in London, by four lions, it is 133ft 6in tall.

## WHY 'DADDY' HILL?

In the 1700s and 1800s there was no aftercare for wounded soldiers or their dependents. Wounds from musket balls would often turn gangrenous, meaning that limbs had to be amputated. Without a leg, or an arm, your career as a soldier would be ended and your chances of finding any work in civilian life were seriously curtailed. All this meant that instead of being able to support a wife and any dependents, the wounded soldier would become dependent himself. Better to be killed outright so that your wife and family would at least be free to seek support elsewhere.

This was a constant fear for soldiers. One of the first generals ever to take this into consideration was the Marquis of Granby who, in the mid-1700s, would often help his favoured old soldiers to set up in business when they were forced to retire from the army. Rowland Hill was another general who cared deeply for the men under his command and went to great lengths to limit the losses his forces suffered in any engagement. He was also known to support those men forced to retire too soon. This treatment of people who, as often as not, were considered cannon-fodder meant that his men trusted him, and indeed loved him. They gave him the nickname *Daddy Hill*.

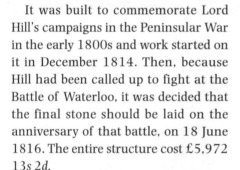

It was built to commemorate Lord Hill's campaigns in the Peninsular War in the early 1800s and work started on it in December 1814. Then, because Hill had been called up to fight at the Battle of Waterloo, it was decided that the final stone should be laid on the anniversary of that battle, on 18 June 1816. The entire structure cost £5,972 13*s* 2*d*.

The column itself is built of Grinshill stone from a quarry a few miles north of Shrewsbury. The statue of Lord Hill standing on the top, however, is made of Coade stone. Coade stone isn't really a stone at all but a ceramic made from a mixture of clay blended with flint and quartz sand. It was invented by Eleanor Coade in the late 1700s and for a long time it was thought that the formula to produce it was lost with her death, although it has now been reproduced. Small decorative pieces made from Coade stone can be seen above doors and windows of buildings all over the country and it was also often used for the production of statues and funerary objects. The statue of Lord Hill is thought to be the largest surviving Coade stone statue.

# AD 1848

# THE EMPTY TOMB

**I**N THE 1700S and 1800s the most dishonourable thing an honourable man could do was to refuse to settle gambling debts. Murder? That could be forgiven. But to renege on your gaming debts, debts owed to your friends and colleagues – that was totally beyond the pale. When an honourable man found himself in this position there were few things he could do – leave the country or commit suicide were about the only options he had.

This was exactly the dilemma faced by Charles Robert Cureton, an officer in the British Army. He therefore decided to fake his own death – and so, one day, he left his clothes on a beach and walked into the sea, in the hope that everyone would assume that he had drowned.

But he didn't drown. Instead, he walked out of the water, a little distance away from where he had abandoned his things, and, dressing in other clothes that he had brought along for the purpose, he walked away to make a new life for himself. Later that same day he came across an army recruiting officer and decided to join up, this time in the ranks.

It was several years later when, on parade one day, he was spotted and recognised by the inspecting officer. And then the whole story came out. Instead of being reviled for what he had done, Cureton was forgiven and instantly promoted within the army. From then on he rose steadily through the ranks until, finally, he became an aide-de-camp to Queen Victoria and Adjutant General of her forces in India.

The tomb you see today under the tower in St Mary's church, however, is empty. Cureton never came back from India but died in the Battle of Ramnagar shortly before he was due to come home to his retirement. It was his fellow officers who arranged to have the memorial tomb erected in his memory. Incidentally, there should be a metal sword in the scabbard that lies on his chest. It disappeared during the Second World War – Shrewsbury people blame American soldiers who were billeted in the town at the time for its disappearance!

SACRED TO THE MEMORY OF
COLONEL C. R. CURETON, C. B. AND A.D.C. TO THE QUEEN.
ADJUTANT GENERAL OF H.M. FORCES IN INDIA.
AND LATE LIEUT. COLONEL COMMANDING THE 16TH LANCERS,
WHO FELL IN AN ENGAGEMENT WITH THE SIKH TROOPS AT RAMNUGGUR.
ON THE 22ND NOVEMBER 1848.
WHEN COMMANDING THE CAVALRY OF THE BRITISH ARMY UNDER GENERAL LORD GOUGH, G.C.B.

THIS MONUMENT IS ERECTED BY HIS COMRADES AND BROTHER OFFICERS IN INDIA
BY WHOM HE WAS HELD AS A SOLDIER IN UNIVERSAL ADMIRATION AND RESPECT.
AND IN LOVE AND ESTEEM AS A FRIEND.

*The magnificent but empty Cureton tomb.*

## ANOTHER ODD GRAVE

Not all gravestones are genuine. Search among the graves in the churchyard of New St Chad's church and you'll find the grave of Ebenezer Scrooge. If you look at this stone carefully, you'll see that there are the markings of an earlier inscription towards the bottom. We have no idea whose name was originally carved here but the stone was recarved at the request of a film crew working in Shrewsbury on a version of *A Christmas Carol* that was released in 1984 and starred George C. Scott as Ebenezer Scrooge.

# DEADLY DR PALMER

## A Poisoner's Last Murder

**W**ILLIAM PALMER WAS a doctor who lived in Rugeley in Staffordshire. Sadly for William, in 1854 his wife died. But every cloud has a silver lining, and the silver lining in this case was that William had not long before taken out a life-insurance policy on his wife. Having paid a premium of only £750, he then received the sum of £13,000. The money was very helpful, allowing William to pay off many of his debts, particularly those he owed to his friend and fellow gambling enthusiast John Parsons Cook. William, however, was an inveterate gambler and before long he was, once again, deeply in debt to Cook.

In the year following his wife's death William took out another life-insurance policy – this time for his brother, Walter – for the sum of £84,000. Walter died and, in view of the sum of money involved, the insurance company decided to send two inspectors to investigate the death. The inspectors discovered that Palmer had been attempting to take out yet another policy, this time on the life of a farmer who was then employed by Dr Palmer.

*Contemporary portrait of William Palmer.*

Suspicious, they recommended that the insurance company should not pay and that further inquiries should be made by the authorities into Walter's death. But nothing happened.

Then, in November of 1855, John Parsons Cook invited William Palmer, along with a number of other friends, to join him in Shrewsbury for the races. They were all betting heavily. Cook won £3,000, but Palmer kept on losing. (Mind you, I can't help but feel that anyone betting on a horse called *The Chicken* deserves to lose.)

After the races a miserable Palmer joined Cook and his friends at the Raven Hotel for celebratory drinks. Cook was drinking heavily and complained at one time that his brandy had burnt his throat. Palmer took a sip of the drink (or pretended to take a sip?) and informed everyone that there appeared to be nothing wrong with it. Soon afterwards Cook was violently sick; he even accused Palmer of putting something in his drink.

The friends returned to Rugeley and Cook appeared to recover from his brief illness. However, a few days later he and Palmer met for coffee and, once again, Cook fell ill. As his doctor, it was inevitable that Palmer should treat Cook. The pills he gave his patient didn't seem to help. Even the little food Cook tried to eat made him vomit. After four days, Cook died in agony, screaming out that he was suffocating to death. Palmer then asked a retired doctor to sign a death certificate which stated that Cook had died from an apoplexy.

Two days after Cook's death his stepfather arrived and started to go through his papers. It appeared that Cook's betting books had been lost – but when he enquired about these, Dr Palmer said that it was irrelevant since, with Cook's death, all bets made between them were null and void.

At the request of Cook's stepfather a post-mortem took place. Palmer was present and, at one point, put the contents of Cook's stomach in a jar for 'safe-

## PALMER'S TOWN/PALMERSTON

All the gory details of the murder trial were described in the newspapers, fascinating the papers' readership, just as such cases do today. Dr William Palmer soon came to be known as the Rugeley Poisoner and, inevitably, the people who lived in the town came to abhor this association with such a notorious case. They decided to petition the Prime Minister for permission to change the town's name. The Prime Minister is said to have agreed with the townspeople that it was an excellent idea. He suggested that they use his own surname as the new name for Rugeley. The Prime Minister's name? Lord Palmerston!

Realising that they were becoming something of a laughing stock, the people of Rugeley quickly dropped their application and decided to wait for another scandal in some other town to grab people's attention instead.

Incidentally, it is said that this story is entirely a myth – but it's a good one, just the same.

*The execution of William Palmer, as it appeared in* Famous Crimes: Past and Present.

keeping'. When the contents were later examined they were found to be of such poor quality that they were of no use. A second post-mortem took place. This time Palmer wrote a letter to the coroner (in which he enclosed £10) asking that a verdict of natural causes should be given.

No actual evidence of poison was found but the coroner was convinced there was a case to answer and stated that there was enough evidence against Palmer to convene a trial. Before the court case began, Palmer's wife was exhumed and antimony was discovered in her organs. In due course other evidence was brought forward, including the fact that Palmer had forged his mother's signature in order to obtain money. Also, a local chemist admitted

selling strychnine to Palmer without noting the sale in his poisons book as he should have done – Palmer had told him he needed it for his dog.

Palmer was found guilty and, in June 1856, 30,000 people went to Stafford Prison to witness his public execution by hanging. It later transpired that Palmer had probably killed quite a number of people other than his wife, his brother and Cook. Likely victims of the Prince of Poisoners included his mother-in-law, four of his children and at least two other people. He should never have started his murderous poisoning of Cook, his last victim, while he was in Shrewsbury – there were too many witnesses who later recalled Cook's complaints about how the brandy had burnt his throat.

# AD 1860

# MURDER IN COTON HILL?

**L**YING IN BED with severe stomach pains, Maria Poulter determined that she would get her revenge on the pub landlord, Richard Jones, who had caused her injuries. Three weeks after a fracas with Jones at the Royal Oak public house on Chester Street, Maria asked a local magistrate to call on her. By this time her injuries had caused her to become bedridden and she was convinced that she was at death's door. If that was the case, she vowed, then she was going to make sure that Jones would suffer too.

Maria told the magistrate of her visit to the Royal Oak pub, where she had bought some ale and a cheese. She described how Richard Jones, finding her there, had accused her son of stealing his eggs. She had denied the accusation; he had then pushed her over and knelt on her as she lay on the floor. Then Jones had hauled her to her feet and, taking her by the neck, had pushed her out of the building so that she fell down the stairs outside. He had then stood by the door, laughing, as his dog bit at the hem of her dress. Maria had managed to get to her feet, and she tried to re-enter the pub in order to retrieve her ale and cheese. Jones had pushed her away once more and, shaken, she had gone home, threatening to get a police summons against the man.

She did not, however, call for the police. Instead, the following day, she had called for a doctor, Dr Burd, to visit her. He found that she was covered in bruises, and had also begun to bleed. The doctor examined Maria and, at first, thought that she might have suffered a miscarriage. Then he decided that her bleeding was probably caused by an internal rupture.

After a couple of days Maria seemed to recover. She left her bed – only to return to it soon afterwards, suffering from severe abdominal pains. A fever took hold and then, four weeks after her argument with Jones, she died.

An inquest was held to determine the cause of her death.

Prior to the inquest, Dr Burd carried out a post-mortem and discovered that the abdominal muscles on Maria Poulter's left side had indeed ruptured, causing a large clot of blood to form within the muscles. He also ascertained

*The Royal Oak, Chester Street.*

that she had not recently miscarried. It seemed obvious to everyone at the inquest that it must have been the rupture that had caused her death – and that the cause of the rupture was the injuries she sustained when Jones pushed her over. Richard Jones should be tried for manslaughter, if not for murder.

Dr Burd, however, disagreed. He insisted that if Jones had merely pushed her over and held her to the floor using his knee it would not have caused such an injury. Instead, he said, the rupture was far more likely to have been self-inflicted by Maria herself when she struggled against Jones. Furthermore, he added, Maria Poulter had then suffered from typhoid fever, probably as a result by her weakened state following the argument with Jones. It was the typhoid fever that had ultimately caused her death, and it was this that he put on her death certificate.

Inevitably, the doctor's comments then meant that the coroner's court passed a verdict stating that Maria Poulter's death was the result of natural causes.

This, not surprisingly, did not satisfy Maria's husband, John, and their friends. Nor was their legal representative, Mr Chandler, happy. Chandler persuaded the Poulter family to take things further and a month later the case came to court. First of all, Maria's written declaration against Jones was read out. Then various witnesses were called. John Poulter described how Maria had walked to his blacksmith's shop and complained at the treatment she had received. When she went to bed, later that day, he saw that her body was covered in bruises. It was he who had called Dr Burd the following day.

Other witnesses were called. They described Maria's sores and her weakening condition. They all insisted that she had been a fit and healthy woman until the day Jones had pushed her over. But Dr Burd continued to insist that the cause of Maria's death was typhoid fever. He repeated the comments he had made at the inquest, insisting that it was Maria Poulter's anger against Richard Jones that prevented her from resting properly and allowing herself to recover. It was typhoid fever, he said, that had killed her.

The court was cleared and the magistrates considered their verdict. They could not agree – and so Richard Jones walked free and was never even tried for manslaughter. So what do you think? Did he cause the death of Maria Poulter, or were natural causes to blame?

# AD 1907

# FATAL RAIL CRASH AT SHREWSBURY STATION

B Y THE EARLY 1900s Shrewsbury had become a major railway junction for lines travelling both east-west and north-south. There was a mixture of both passenger and freight trains and some, such as the mail trains, combined the two.

In the early hours of the morning of 15 October 1907, without any warning, a 400-ton mail train came racing into Shrewsbury station at 60mph, smashing into everything in its path. The results were disastrous.

An inquiry was held immediately afterwards. In those days, immediately meant immediately – it took place on the day after the crash. One person attending the inquiry was a then still relatively unknown David Lloyd George.

It was ascertained at the inquiry that the driver must have fallen asleep in his cab. Woken suddenly, he must have realised that he was coming into the station too fast and slammed on the brakes – causing the train to derail. There seemed to be no other explanation since the weather was fine and no faults could be found with the train itself. One thing that did come out of

the inquiry was that the train had been eight minutes late leaving Crewe. It was therefore assumed that the driver might have been travelling faster than normal in an effort to catch up with his time.

Altogether eighteen people were killed, including the driver, and the results of the inquiry remained largely conjecture. Other fatalities included three postal workers who had been working in the mail coach at the time of the crash; the fireman from the train; four members of staff from the station; and eleven passengers. A further sixty-seven people were injured, although many were able to go home after receiving treatment at the nearby hospital.

But that wasn't the end of the story. Both the driver, Samuel Martin, and the fireman, Frederick Fletcher, were from Crewe, and the fact that they were both rapidly made into scapegoats infuriated other railwaymen at Crewe. They promptly carried out their own investigation. It was ascertained that, although it was agreed that the train was eight minutes late leaving Crewe, it had made up that lost time before it reached Shrewsbury. So there would

*The most fascinating thing about this postcard (apart from the message on the back) is the postmark – it was posted before 11 a.m. on the day after the accident.*

have been no need to travel at such speed as it came into the station. Moreover, the post-mortem that was carried out on Samuel Martin (who had been scalded to death) and on Frederick Fletcher proved that they had not been drinking, and so it was less likely that both of them could have fallen asleep. The final piece of evidence was that Martin appeared to have reversed the engine before the crash, which other railwaymen agreed seemed to imply that the brakes on the engine had failed.

As a result of their investigations, the Crewe railwaymen passed a resolution in protest at the official inquiry's results and, shortly afterwards, a similar resolution was passed by railwaymen in Liverpool.

Of the eighteen fatalities, three were postal workers who would have been working in the travelling post office at the time; there were four members of station staff amongst the dead. The other people killed were all passengers, some of them from Shrewsbury.

*The gravestone of Stephen Hodgson, killed in the accident.*

At the time of the inquiry, however, not all the victims had been identified. For example, one woman was described in the paper the next day whose only piece of identification was that she had 'a ticket for St Ives'. Another, a man, was described as being 'dressed as a sailor, unrecognisable, between 35 and 40 years of age'.

It's not known exactly how many people were on the train at the time of the crash – probably around 100 – but sixty-seven had to be treated in hospital with injuries ranging from cuts and bruises to broken bones and, in one case, a spinal injury.

## OTHER RAILWAY FATALITIES

Although the railway accident in October 1907 was the worst ever to occur in Shropshire, it was not the only time when there were fatalities on the railway system, and not all of these were caused by working steam locomotives. Even before the first train arrived in Shrewsbury, there had been accidents.

Shrewsbury railway station lies at the northern end of the town where, thanks to the curve of the River Severn that surrounds the town, there is only a relatively narrow strip of land. Consequently, not only do the platforms for the station itself extend along bridges over the river but also, because of the way that the river meanders, the line crosses another bridge to the east of the town known as the Belvedere Railway Bridge. It was while this bridge was being constructed in 1846 that two workmen fell into the river and drowned. Then, soon afterwards, a cutting was being dug for the same stretch of line, close to Shrewsbury Abbey, when the bank caved in, trapping another workman. He suffocated before he could be dug out.

The station finally opened for business in 1849. Three years later, the first accident to involve a steam locomotive occurred.

## DISASTER POETRY

A couple of days after the crash, an anonymous five-verse poem about the disaster was printed in the *Shrewsbury Chronicle*. It was the work of a young woman who lived on the outskirts of the town, in Meole Brace. Her name was Mary Meredith, and the poem had been submitted to the paper (without her knowledge) by her brother. It's thought, therefore, to be the first published work by the Shropshire novelist better known under her married name, Mrs Mary Webb.

A passenger engine, the *Mazeppa*, was parked in sheds alongside Abbey Foregate whilst a leaky valve was repaired. The repair was completed and the engineer who had done the work left for home. Only a few minutes later, the next shift arrived – to find that the engine had disappeared.

It turned out that the engineer had left the locomotive in gear. Once the steam pressure built up, the train started to move all on its own. A workman on the line noticed that it was moving without a driver and raised the alarm but it was already too late. The *Mazeppa* travelled all the way to Donnington, several miles away, before it finally came to a stop – by crashing into the back of another train. One passenger was killed.

Then, in 1875, a train driver was killed in another accident which also began in Abbey Foregate. On this occasion a goods train shunted three wagons which proceeded to run out of control, heading straight for another train pulling fourteen heavy wagons. The driver of the second train didn't stand a chance and was crushed between the bunker and firebox of his engine.

The last occasion on which there was a fatal railway accident took place in January 1965 at Coton Hill. It involved another freight train that ran out of control, this time pulling forty-six wagons and weighing a total of 775 tons. The driver attempted to brake, but the train derailed and smashed into a signal box – killing the signalman who was on duty.

## THE GHOST THAT HAUNTS SHREWSBURY STATION

Strangely enough, the man who haunts the station was not killed in a railway accident. It was January 1887 and there had been a heavy fall of snow, covering the country from northern Wales to Derbyshire. Roads were blocked, sheep were lost in snowdrifts, and few people were about. But some still ventured to travel on the railways and, to serve those passengers arriving at Shrewsbury station, there was one horse-drawn cab waiting for hire – sheltering under the metal awning to the side of the station as it did so. Because there was only one cab there at the time, there was therefore room for a coal merchant to take shelter too.

Suddenly, without warning, the weight of the snow on the awning caused the entire structure to collapse. The waiting cab was demolished, and its horse injured, but fortunately the cabbie escaped injury. The coal merchant, however, was not so lucky. He was killed instantly.

Ever since then the coal merchant has haunted the area.

The accident was described in the *Illustrated London News* of the day. The writer pointed out that the accident took place at 'half-past three in the afternoon, the hour at which the cab-horses are usually fed, or thirty or forty persons might otherwise have been under the roof when it fell.'

# AD 1917

# WALTER NAPLETON STONE VC

**T**HE NAME WALTER Napleton Stone VC is listed on a war memorial in St Mary's church in Shrewsbury.

In fact, we know quite a bit about Stone. He was born in Blackheath, in London, in 1891, the son of a solicitor. There was obviously money in the family because, although he was the fifth son in a large family, his father could still afford to have him educated at Harrow; from there he went on to Pembroke College, Cambridge.

He never gained his degree. Instead, by the age of twenty-five he was an Acting Captain in the Royal Fusiliers and was serving on the Western Front in France. On 30 November 1917 he was in command of an outpost 1,000 yards in front of the main line, from where he was observing enemy movements. Seeing the enemy massing for an attack, he stayed at his post, sending back vital information to his headquarters.

Eventually he was commanded to withdraw all his men and remain with a rearguard to cover their escape. Unfortunately, the German attack developed unexpectedly quickly and,

although he managed to send three platoons to safety, he and the rearguard found themselves isolated. There was no escape – yet, well aware of the danger of his position, Stone continued to send back information about the enemy's movements, thus saving the front line from disaster. At times, despite the severe bombardment of their position, Stone could be seen standing on the parapet so that he could get a better view, the telephone in his hand, passing on his information. At the last possible minute, he ordered that the telephone line should be cut. He – and the men with him – were all killed, Stone being shot through the head.

*Stone's memorial in St Mary's church.*

## THE KING'S (SHROPSHIRE) LIGHT INFANTRY

The regiment most closely associated with Shropshire and Shrewsbury is the King's (Shropshire) Light Infantry, or KSLI. Like so many British regiments, its name and county links have changed many times over the years. However, this regiment could be said to have been founded in 1755, when it was known as the 53rd Foot, although a second infantry regiment, the 85th, later came to be amalgamated with it.

The regiment's first foreign tour was to be in Canada, where men were sent in 1776 to relieve Quebec. Here the regiment stayed for some ten years. At one point, whilst under heavy attack, an officer cut down the regiment's Colours and wrapped them around his body, under his uniform, to prevent them being captured by the enemy. Renamed The Shropshire Regiment in 1782, it moved to Bridgnorth after it returned from Canada.

In the early 1800s the regiment saw service in the Peninsular War – it was there that the future Lord Hill came to prominence – and they also served in America in the war of 1812, coming soon afterwards to be known as The Duke of York's Own Regiment of Light Infantry. Elevation to become The King's Light Infantry came as a result of an incident in 1821, when King George IV was attacked by a mob during a visit to Brighton: it was soldiers from the 85th regiment who rescued him.

The 1800s saw the regiment, besides taking part in battles such as Talavera, Salamanca and Vittoria, go further afield to India, where it took part in the relief of Lucknow. In one action at Lucknow four Victoria Crosses were awarded to soldiers in the KSLI. The regiment also fought in Africa, taking part in the recapture of Khartoum and, later, in the Boer War. At one point a battalion was sent as far as Hong Kong – where, rather than fighting a battle, they were involved in fighting an epidemic of plague which killed over 2,000 Chinese people.

But, of course, it was the First World War which was to see the KSLI involved in the worst fighting, with eight of its eleven battalions serving overseas. War broke out in August 1914. The first battalion arrived in France the following month, soon after which they were caught up in the first battle of Ypres. They were subsequently to be involved in the battles of the Somme, Cambrai, and Passchendaele – to name just a few. Altogether, various battalions in the KSLI were awarded sixty battle honours during the First World War.

---

A very brave man, who deserves a fitting memorial, especially since his body was never found by the British – he has no known grave.

But why should he be listed on a memorial in Shrewsbury? So far as anyone knows, he never came near the town or had any association with it whatsoever. So why is he here? It has been suggested that his parents moved to the town in 1914, but there seems to be no mention of them on any town records. It's all a bit of a mystery.

Then there's another mystery on the memorial stone in St Mary's. It lists his awards as being VC, DSO, MC (Victoria Cross, Distinguished Service Order, Military Cross). But according to the Royal Fusiliers Museum he was never given the last two awards... A mystery waiting to be solved!

# THE OLD LIE

## Dulce et Decorum Est

**P**ICTURE THE SCENE. The year is 1918. The month is November. The date is the eleventh. Suddenly, at eleven o'clock in the morning, all the church bells up and down the country start to ring out the joyous news: after four hideous years, peace has at last been declared. Over 15 million people had been killed as a result of the war, and a further 20 million wounded. But, finally, the war to end all wars had ended. Everyone could now breathe more easily. Soon all those who had survived the horror would begin to trickle home, your beloved son amongst them.

Then, only an hour later, the postman calls and brings the news. Your son was shot and killed just a week before – on 4 November.

This is exactly what happened to one family in Monkmoor Road in Shrewsbury, the home of Wilfred Owen's family.

Wilfred Owen had been born in Oswestry in 1893. From there his family moved to Birkenhead before coming to Shrewsbury in 1910, where he finished his formal education at Shrewsbury

Technical College. He wanted to go on to university but, although he passed the entrance examinations, he did not get a high enough mark to enable him to be given a scholarship. His family could not afford to pay for him to go so he had to give up the idea of becoming a full-time student. It did not mean,

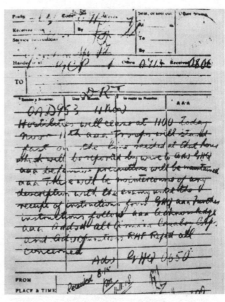

*The famous telegram sent to the various fronts on 11 November. 'Hostilities will cease at 11.00 today,' it begins. It was a message that Wilfred Owen was never to receive.*

*News of the Armistice at home and abroad. At the top we see the troops reading the telegram printed overleaf; above we see the royal family on the balcony of Buckingham Palace, cheered by thousands of Londoners who have gathered, as they did in Shrewsbury, to celebrate the end of the war.*

however, that he gave up the idea entirely: instead, he worked as a lay assistant to the vicar of Dunsden, near Reading, in order to help pay for him to attend classes at the university there. Then for a time he worked in Bordeaux, in France, teaching English, and he was there when the First World War broke out in 1914.

In 1915 he enlisted, full – as so many men of his generation were at the time – of optimism in a cause worth fighting for. Once he had been sent to France in 1917, however, it soon became evident from his letters home that his feelings had undergone a change. After being blown into the sky by a mortar and then, soon afterwards, becoming trapped in a German dugout for some days, he suffered from shellshock and was sent back to England to recuperate. It was then that he met the poet Siegfried Sassoon, who was to have an immense influence on Owen's work.

In 1918, Wilfred Owen was deemed to be fit enough to return to the front. Shortly after his arrival in France, he and the Royal Engineers under his command were ordered to erect a pontoon bridge to enable the soldiers to cross the Sambre-Oise Canal, so that they could capture and destroy German-held machine guns on the eastern side. Standing in the open, encouraging his men in their work, Owen was a perfect target and, on 4 November, exactly a week before peace was declared, he was shot in the head. He died instantly.

Wilfred Owen's poetry only came to be known to a wider world after his death. When, in 1985, a memorial to First World War poets (of whom Owen must rank amongst the greatest) was unveiled in Westminster Abbey's Poet's Corner, the inscription chosen was *My subject is War, and the pity of War. The Poetry is in the Pity*. This quote was from the Preface to a book of his poems.

## 'I AM THE ENEMY YOU KILLED, MY FRIEND'

A strange-looking memorial, which sits in the churchyard of Shrewsbury Abbey, represents a pontoon bridge of the type that Owen was helping to construct when he was shot and killed.

Along one side are words that come from one of his most famous poems, *Strange Meeting*. The poem tells the imaginary story of two soldiers who, coming up against each other in the battlefields of the Western Front, somehow manage to kill each other. They then meet in the hallway to the next world, where they fall into conversation – only to discover that, had they not met as enemies, they could have been good friends, sharing so many interests and beliefs.

One of Owen's finest and most devastating poems is reprinted below. It comes from the 1994 Chatto & Windus volume *The War Poems of Wilfred Owen*, with grateful acknowledgement to the editor of that volume, Jon Stallworthy.

### THE CHANCES

I 'mind as how the night before that show
Us five got talkin'; we was in the know.
'Ah well,' says Jimmy, and he's seen some scrappin',
'There ain't more than five things as can happen, –
You get knocked out; else wounded, bad or cushy;
Scuppered; or nowt except you're feelin' mushy.'

One of us got the knock-out, blown to chops;
One lad was hurt, like, losin' both his props;
And one – to use the word of hypocrites –
Had the misfortune to be took by Fritz.
Now me, I wasn't scratched, praise God Almighty,
Though next time please I'll thank Him for a blighty.
But poor old Jim, he's livin' and he's not;
He reckoned he'd five chances, and he had:
He's wounded, killed, and pris'ner, all the lot,
The flamin' lot all rolled in one. Jim's mad.

# AD 1940

# BATTLE OF BRITAIN

## The Story of Eric 'Sawn-Off' Lock

'Never in the field of human conflict was so much owed by so many to so few.'
*Sir Winston Churchill, 20 August 1940*

The Battle of Britain was mainly fought in the skies over south-eastern England, and little evidence of it was seen over the county of Shropshire. However, those who came to be known later as *the few* came from all parts – and one of them was a certain Eric Stanley Lock, who was born in Bayston Hill, just outside Shrewsbury.

Eric Lock's father ran a quarrying and farming business and it was into this line of work that the young man went on leaving school. It was obvious to many in the latter part of the 1930s that war was in the offing and, knowing that he was likely to be called up, Lock decided to join the Royal Air Force Volunteer Reserve in the hope that, should war break out, he would then become a fighter pilot.

This is exactly what happened. He enlisted on 1 September 1939 and trained as a Spitfire pilot before being posted in May of 1940 to join No. 41 Squadron, which was then based at Catterick, in North Yorkshire. Within weeks the Battle of Britain had begun and, to begin with, it had little effect on those pilots in Yorkshire who were tasked with flying regular patrols away from the main battle zone. Flying over northern England and protecting its

---

### THE FIRST BRITISH ARMY FATALITY OF THE SECOND WORLD WAR

The first soldier killed in action in the Second World War was a soldier serving with the KSLI. His name was Cpl Thomas W. Priday, and he was killed by a landmine when leading a patrol towards the German lines. He had been guarding the French Maginot Line. The date was 9 December 1939.

## A BOMB FALLS ON SHREWSBURY

Shrewsbury, and indeed all of Shropshire, survived the Second World War relatively unscathed. But that is not to say there were no bomb attacks. These were probably the result of a German bomber returning from a trip to Merseyside. Realising, when he saw a light below, that he had one or two bombs left on board that he could drop, the pilot released his remaining munitions. Some people were killed in Bridgnorth as a result of an air raid and others in Ellesmere. On one occasion a searchlight unit in the village of Hodnet was attacked: everyone on duty there was killed.

In Shrewsbury a man returned to his house on the outskirts of the town. He had been drinking rather heavily that evening and so, instead of going to bed (and perhaps checking that all the lights were off), he stumbled to the couch downstairs and passed out. He was the only one to survive when the house was hit by a bomb later that night.

coastline was not entirely without its excitements, however. Lock got his first kill on 15 August when he downed a twin-engined Messerschmitt over the North Sea.

Meanwhile, the RAF was suffering from severe losses further south and within a few weeks, 'Sawn-Off' Lock and his squadron were posted to RAF Hornchurch in Essex. (He was nicknamed Sawn-Off, incidentally, because he was so much shorter than his fellows.)

By September 1940 the Battle of Britain was raging. There were regular Luftwaffe raids on London and towns all over southern England. It was only two days after his arrival at Hornchurch that Lock got his next kill (or kills). Flying over the Thames Estuary he shot down two Luftwaffe bombers and then was hit himself, receiving an injury to his leg. At this point he would have been wise to have gone back to his base but, instead, he decided to fight back, and as a result of brilliant manoeuvring managed to

## THE YANKS ARE COMING

In January 1942, less than two months after America entered the war, the first Americans arrived in Shropshire. Before long there was a common complaint by the locals in Shrewsbury that they could never enter a pub without it being 'full of Yanks'.

By the end of that year there were some 40,000 US troops stationed in Shropshire alone. When you consider that the present-day population of Shropshire is somewhere around 400,000, and that, during the war years, many of the local men had been sent elsewhere, it does not take much imagination to consider the effect these GIs had on the local population…

force the attacking Messerschmitt 109 into a position from where he could fire on it. The plane exploded in mid-air. That day Lock landed his damaged Spitfire, having shot down three enemy aircraft.

The next day Lock was up in the air once again, despite the injury to his leg. He shot down a Junkers bomber and within days he downed yet more aircraft. In all, within one week, Eric Lock destroyed eight enemy planes. He was awarded the DFC (Distinguished Flying Cross) for displaying 'great vigour and determination in pressing home his attacks'. Already his reputation as an ace fighter pilot had begun.

By the time that the Battle of Britain was deemed to be over, at the end of October 1940, Flight Lieutenant Eric Lock had become the most successful British-born pilot in the battle. He had shot down 16.5 German aircraft – that half an aircraft was a kill he shared with another pilot.

The Battle of Britain may have been won but the war in the air went on, as the RAF fought to protect Britain during the regular raids in the years that followed. 'Sawn-Off' Lock continued to fly. He suffered from several near misses, the worst one taking place in November 1940 when his plane received a direct hit from a Messerschmitt. On this

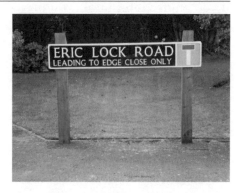

*The road now named after Eric Lock.*

occasion Lock crashed to the ground. He landed some distance from help and was trapped, wounded, in his cockpit for nearly two hours before he was found and carried to safety.

It's not known exactly what happened to Eric Lock in the end. In August 1941, he vanished – he had been engaged in a bombing raid over France, and it must be assumed that he was shot down. His plane was never found, and so he has no known grave.

Eric 'Sawn-Off' Lock had been awarded the DFC twice and the DSO. Altogether he shot down some twenty-six enemy aircraft so that, although he died four years before the war even ended, he was still just outside the top ten of the RAF highest scorers of downed aircraft for the whole of the Second World War.

## JAM AND THE WI

One curious statistic is that during the war years more jam was produced by the Women's Institute in Shropshire than in any other county in England – apparently they produced 92,642lbs. I want to know who was counting.

If you enjoyed this book, you may also be interested in…

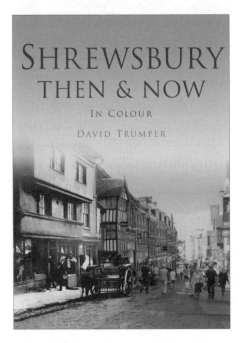

## Shrewsbury Then & Now

DAVID TRUMPER

*Shrewsbury Then & Now* is a superb collection photographs of the town, compiled by local historian and well-known author David Trumper. Scenes of yesteryear are contrasted with modern colour views to show what has been lost – and what remains. This book offers an insight into people's daily lives and living conditions in the town, and the nature of the photographs, and David Trumper's informative captions, show the sometimes drastic changes which have taken place in the name of progress. Drawing on detailed local knowledge of the community and illustrated with a wealth of images, this book will delight residents and visitors alike.

978 0 7524 6405 3

## Haunted Shrewsbury

MARTIN WOOD

From heart-stopping accounts of poltergeists to first-hand encounters with spectres, this book will appeal to anyone who wants to know more about Shrewsbury's mysterious history. Discover the headless apparition at the castle gates, ghostly monks from the abbey church and a whole family of spirits in Milk Street. Martin Wood, a town crier and toastmaster, has had an interest in ghosts for many years, and for the past ten years has been leading evening tours of Shrewsbury, looking at haunted sites in the town.

978 0 7524 4303 4

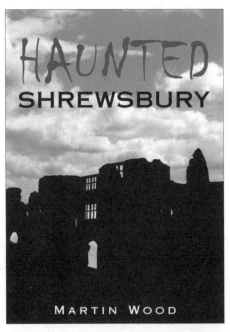